Inside you will find...

LOCAL Recipes

by

LOCAL Fishermen

made exclusively with

LOCAL Catch.

"Local is Fresh and Fresh is Best!"

Welcome to the bounty of

The Fisherman's Table!

The Fisherman's Table

Enjoy the bounty!
Laura Blackwell

The Fisherman's Table

Recipes caught from the Newport sea

by Laura Blackwell

with contributions by the Fishermen of Newport
page illustrations by Sean Warren
and cover art by Mary Adiletta

TOURO STREET BOOKS
NEWPORT, RHODE ISLAND

The Fisherman's Table
Recipes caught from the Newport sea
Copyright © 2012 Laura E. Blackwell
All rights reserved.
"Lobster Trap Table" graphic is a registered trademark of Touro Street Books.

This book or any portion thereof may not be reproduced in any manner whatsoever without the express written permission of the publisher except for the use of brief quotations in a book review.

Published by:	Touro Street Books
	3 Whitfield Place
	Newport, Rhode Island, 02840

Orders at:	www.FishermansTable.com

ISBN-10: 0-615-66647-7
ISBN-13: 978-0-615-66647-1

Font: 'Handwriting-Draft' © 2011 'Fontscafe.com'
Font: 'Shonar Bangla' © 2008 The Monotype Corporation
Font: 'Old Newspaper Type' © Manfred Klein 2001-2008
Font: 'Lewis Carroll' created 2002 by Jaz and licensed as freeware.

Cover illustration and "Lobster Trap Table," graphic by Mary Adiletta.
Page illustrations by Sean Warren excluding "Lobster Trap Table."
Back cover illustration by Sean Warren.

Printed in the United States of America
First Printing, 2012

*for Eric,
who brings home the fish*

About the Fisherman's Table...

Every morning...

...the sun rises over Aquidneck Island. Before the first rays hit land, Newport's fishing fleet is out seeking the ocean's fruits. The 'catch' is never predictable, but always fresh, making the fisherman's table heavy with seafood and creativity. Lobster, crab, conch, clams, squid and any number of 'swimming' fish grace these waters. The ways to prepare them are infinite.

For example...

...as of this writing, there are 17 boats in Newport's lobster fishing fleet, not to speak of Newport's squidders, clam diggers, gill-netters, fish-trawlers, etc. That means there are 17 authentic, absolutely correct ways to make a 'Newport Lobster Roll.' (Russell swears by diced cucumbers rather than celery. Eric is a fan of relish. John uses minced garlic while his wife prefers bell peppers. Denny and Nancy argue over whether or not lobster meat should ever make it near a food processor, while Robby won't let any mayonnaise other than Hellman's touch his lobster, ever. As. God. Is. His. Witness.)

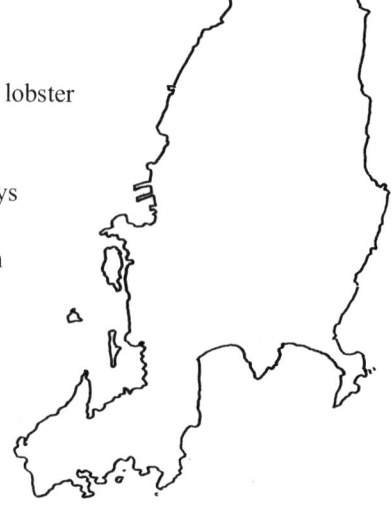

However...

...even in something as personal as a lobster roll, we've uncovered some steadfast 'fisherman' themes:

1. The meat from one whole lobster must go into each roll –

    No Skimping! Seafood is the one item guaranteed to be abundant in a fisherman's house. Thus, their recipes all tend to begin with phrases like 'double the lobster meat,' or, 'go heavy on the clams,' creating the type of meals seafood lovers dream about, but rarely get in restaurants.
2. Fishermen take the time to grill the hot dog roll. Fishing is not an easy profession, and one that stresses doing things right, or not at all. In the same vein, fishermen don't concern themselves with much nonsense. When a specialty ingredient or extra step truly 'adds' to a dish – they use it. But when an onion from the red bag will do equally as well as a shallot...they'll go onion every time.
3. The lobsters must be fresh and from the local waters. Local is fresh and fresh is best. Lobstermen buy squid from a local guy – or they don't eat squid. Simple.

Following those themes...

...the recipes on these pages tend to be packed with local seafood and local flavor. By default, they're also relatively healthy. Deep-fried fritters and heavily battered clam cakes have their place, and we feel that that place is in a restaurant; we don't know a lot of fishermen who head home to deep-fry pounds of batter. Similarly, salt is used rarely, as the ocean salts its own. You won't find any mention of shrimp, salmon or tilapia, as they are not caught in the local waters, though they remain prominent on local menus. You will find some 'from the land' recipes for desserts that can be made with wild or farmed 'fruits of the island.' They pair beautifully with local 'fruits of the ocean...'

Again...

...there are infinite ways to cook anything. Within these pages you will find

trusted, tested, tasty

ways to prepare Aquidneck Island's bountiful gifts, both from the water and the land. Some recipes come directly from individual fishermen. Some from local custom. Some from Laura's kitchen via Eric's plate. All are made with 'catch' local to Newport, RI. We hope you enjoy the local flavors. We do. Every night.

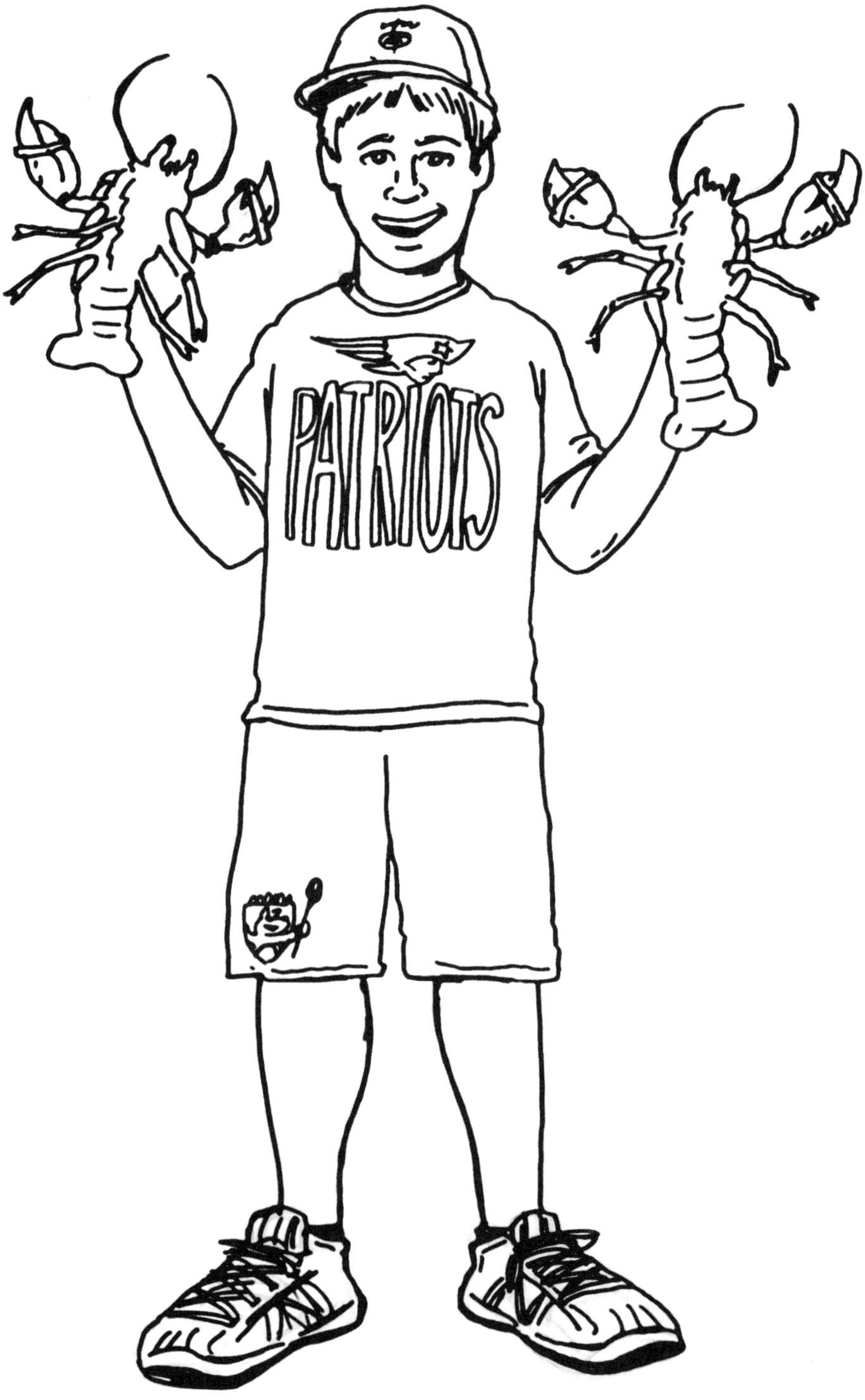
PATRIOTS

Local Recipes, Local Flavor...

Clams 1-21

Clam Chowder 3-Ways 4
Clam Dip 6
Linguine with Clam Sauce 8
Mule Hog Stuffies 10
Mushroom and Bacon Stuffies 12
Portuguese Littlenecks 14
Steamer Boil 16
Steaming Big Clams for Re-Cooking 18
White Clam Pizza 20

Conch 23-31

Coconut Conch Salsa 26
Conch Salad 28
Jamaican Conch Soup 30

Crabs 33-45

Christmas Crab & Broccoli Soup 36
Crab Boil 38
Crab Cakes with Chipotle Mayo 40
Marinated Crab 42
Rock Crab Dip 43
Sand Crab & Roasted Corn Chowder 44

Fish 47-69

Blackfish Cioppino 50
Fast Baked Fish, Potato & Vegetable 52
Fish Stock 54
Fish Tacos 56
Flounder Francese 58
Grilled Whole Fish 60
Portuguese Baked Blackfish 62
Portuguese Fish Chowder 64
Sweet & Sour Monkfish Stir-Fry 66
Sweet Potato Fish Cakes 68

Lobster 71-93
Basic Steamed Lobster 74
Char-grilled Lobster Bullets 76
Lobster & Crab Bisque 78
Lobster 'Fra Diablo' 80
Lobsterman's Mac 'n' Cheese 82
Lobsterman's Pie 84
Lobster or Crab Stock 86
Lobster Scampi 88
Lobster Stuffed Lobster 90
Soft Lobster Boats 92

Mussels, Oysters, Scallops and Squid 95-109
'Chinese 5-Spice' Calmari 98
Grilled Oysters 'Especial' 100
Newport Scallops 102
Red Curried Mussels 104
Ricotta Stuffed Baby Squid 106
Tequila Lime Grilled Calamari 108

'Catch' from the Land 111-123
Bramble Cobbler 114
Rhubarb Crisp 116
Side-of-the-Road Apple Pie 118
Strawberry Shortcake 120
Very Blueberry Corn Muffins 122

About the Author and Illustrators I

Acknowledgements II

About Clams...

Delicious local clams are lurking under the sand, in the muck, and near the rocks all over Aquidneck Island. Clams you dig with your hands...clams you find with your toes...with the Quahog (pronounced: Koh-Hog) as the official shellfish of Rhode Island! RI residents are able to catch a 'half bushel' of clams a day without a license, making them a big part of local culture. Ask any local about his recipe for stuffies or chowder and be ready for an earful...

The Local Catch

There are three main species that we harvest: soft shell (Steamers), white roundish hard-shell (Quahog), and skinnier huge hard-shell (Surf Clams). Local clams are fished recreationally and commercially. They are briny and delicious and important to the ocean's ecosystem, serving as living filters for the sea. For this reason, clams should only be taken in approved areas, both to protect them, and to protect you! The baby ones (less than an inch thick at the hinge) should be left behind to grow into next summer's harvest!

Which is which?

Steamers, or 'Soft Shell' clams *(Mya arenaria)* are sweet and tender, have a fair amount of natural sand in them, and are almost always eaten on their own, dipped in butter. They live in mud and are most often harvested with a hand rake with long skinny tines.

Quahogs or 'Hard Shell' clams *(Mercenaria mercenaria)* are less sandy as a rule. They are all individually referred to by names explaining their size. 1-2 inchers are called **'Littlenecks'** and are great at a raw bar or served cooked in the shell. **'Cherrystones'** are the next size up: 2-3 inches. These are tender and great to chop up in pasta, etc. What people think of as **'Quahogs'** are the big boys: 3-unlimited inches. They can be chewy and are great for stuffies, clamcakes and chowder. Recreational 'Quahoggers' use a rake with a long pole and a basket to get clams from their rocky, sandy home. The word 'Quahog' itself came from the Narragansett Indians – some of the island's first fishermen.

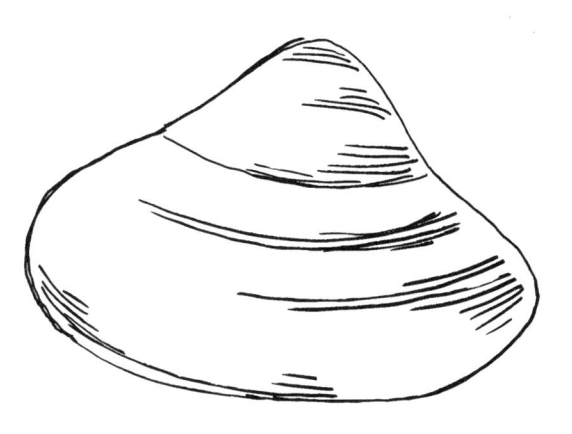

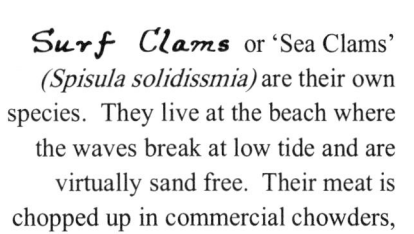

Surf Clams or 'Sea Clams' *(Spisula solidissmia)* are their own species. They live at the beach where the waves break at low tide and are virtually sand free. Their meat is chopped up in commercial chowders, stuffies, and to make fried clam strips. They yield a little less meat than a similar sized Quahog but are by far the easiest clam to get. The most effective tools to find Surf Clams are your toes. No kidding!

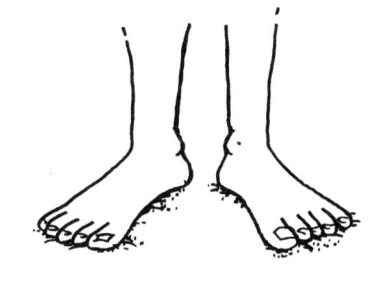

Kitchen Must:
Get all the sand out.

Clam 'Math'

6-8 3-4 inch Quahogs weigh 3 pounds and yield 1 cup meat
6-8 4-5 inch Surf Clams yield 1 cup meat
10-12 Cherrystones yield 1 cup meat
15-20 whole Steamers come in one pound.

Clam Chowder 3-Ways	4
Clam Dip	6
Linguine with Clam Sauce	8
Mule Hog Stuffies	10
Mushroom & Bacon Stuffies	12
Portuguese Littlenecks	14
Steamer Boil	16
Steaming Big Clams for Re-Cooking	18
White Clam Pizza	20

Clam Chowder 3-Ways

Like lobster rolls and stuffies, Rhodies all have their own way of making chowder. Some folks swear it should be creamy. Some swear it should be clear. Some crazies think it should be red...though they're clearly not from here... Here's how to create clammy, healthy-ish versions of all three.

The Catch

12-16 3-4 inch Quahogs
OR 20-24 Cherrystones
OR 12-16 4-5 inch Surf Clams
  (2 cups clam meat)
4 cups clam juice

The Groceries

8-12 ounces salt pork
4 stalks celery, diced
2 onions, diced
2 cloves garlic, minced
2 medium potatoes, diced
½ teaspoon dill and/or thyme
¼ teaspoon black pepper

The Extras

oyster crackers for serving
2 cups heavy cream for 'New England Style' and optional 4 Tablespoons cornstarch
2 cups marinara for 'Manhattan Style' and dash red pepper flakes

The How To

- STEAM and CLEAN clams according to STEAMING BIG CLAMS FOR RE-COOKING (page 18). STRAIN and SAVE 4 cups juice.
- CHOP clams into ¼ inch chunks either by hand, with kitchen scissors or preferably, by a quick pulse in a food processor. SET ASIDE.
- SLICE the 'rind' off of the salt pork, if there is one. DICE salt pork into ¼ inch cubes. If part of it is totally white fat only and that bothers you, you can throw some out. Make sure at least 8 ounces make it into the pot.
- HEAT salt pork over medium heat in a big pot until fat renders and it gets golden brown all over, about 5 minutes. Pieces should be half of their starting size. It may stick to the bottom of the pot and that is okay, so long as it doesn't burn. (Some people now discard these pork crackles, keeping only the liquid fat. We feel like that's a waste – who doesn't like a little bacon in their chowder?)
- ADD celery and onion and COOK until onion is translucent, about 3 minutes. USE this time to scrape up brown stuff from the bottom.
- ADD garlic and cook for 1 minute.
- ADD clam juice, potatoes, and spices.
- DECIDE what 'style' of chowder you are making.
    - If making clear 'Rhode Island-Style' chowder – ADD 4 cups water and SIMMER 20 minutes. ADD clams. SIMMER 10 minutes.
    - If making 'New England-Style' creamy chowder, ADD 2 cups water and SIMMER 20 minutes. Then ADD clams and 2 cups heavy cream and SIMMER 10 minutes. (If 'thick' chowder is desired, you can mix 4 tablespoons of cornstarch into cold cream before adding. Stirring is then required.)
    - If making 'Manhattan-Style' red chowder, ADD 2 cups water, 2 cups marinara sauce and a dash red pepper flakes and SIMMER 20 minutes. ADD clams. SIMMER 10 minutes.
- SERVE with oyster crackers and remember to SCOOP clams from bottom.

Yield: 2½ quarts chowder.
Kitchen Time: 50 minutes.
In Season: Year-round.

Clam Dip
– Bob's way

Makes potato chips disappear...

The Catch
6-8 3-4 inch Quahogs
OR 10-12 Cherrystones
OR 6-8 4-5 inch Surf Clams
   (1 cup meat)
1-2 Tablespoons clam juice

The Groceries
8 ounces light cream cheese, room temperature
double dash Worcestershire sauce

The Extras
kettle-style potato chips

The How To

- STEAM and CLEAN clams according to STEAMING BIG CLAMS FOR RE-COOKING (page 18), but let them open all the way so they are fully cooked. CHOP clams.
- MIX cream cheese and Worcestershire sauce with mixer until combined and 'creamy.'
- ADD clams and MIX, gradually ADDING clam juice until it is a 'dipping' consistency...smooth, but not soupy.

Yield: Appetizer.
Kitchen Time: 5 minutes.
In Season: Year-round.

Linguine with Clam Sauce

- Uncle Jim's way

This is a relatively healthy, flavorful version of a classic dish. Rather than a thick butter sauce...this version focuses on the clam!

The Catch

6-8 3-4 inch Quahogs
OR 10-12 Cherrystones
OR 6-8 4-5 inch Surf Clams
    (1 cup meat)
2 cups clam juice, from
    steaming clams
optional: 36 Littlenecks,
    scrubbed

The Groceries

2-6 Tablespoons olive oil
8 cloves garlic, minced (this is
    not the recipe to be cheap
    on the garlic)
dash red pepper flakes
2 Tablespoons white wine
1 handful fresh parsley,
    chopped
1 pound linguine
black pepper to taste
1 lemon, wedged

The Extras

fresh crusty bread

The How To

- STEAM and CLEAN clams according to **STEAMING BIG CLAMS FOR RE-COOKING** (page 18).
- CHOP clams and SET ASIDE, including all the good brown stuff. PREPARE chopped ingredients. This sauce moves quickly!
- BOIL salted water for pasta. When it boils, COOK pasta until 'al dente.'

Meanwhile make the sauce...

- HEAT 2-8 tablespoons olive oil in a skillet with tall sides. (The more oil you use, the 'thicker' your sauce will be and the more it will stick to the noodles. This is a personal choice.)
- ADD the garlic and red pepper flakes and COOK about 1 minute until it is aromatic but not brown. If you brown it – throw it out and start again.
- ADD white wine, clam broth, chopped clams and parsley.
- IF your Littlenecks are scrubbed and free of sand, ADD them. (If they are sandy, steam them in a different pot and give them a quick rinse before adding at the very end.)
- SIMMER sauce until Littlenecks are all the way open, or, if no Littlenecks, 5 minutes.
- TOSS the sauce including Littlenecks and 'al dente' linguine. ADD black pepper to taste.
- GARNISH with lemon wedges and SERVE with fresh bread to soak up the sauce!

> **Fisherman's Tip**
> *A wire brush makes scrubbing littlenecks super easy.*

Yield: Dinner for 6.
Kitchen Time: 15 minutes, plus prepping clams.
In Season: Year-round.

Mule Hogs

by Robby Braman

Every Rhode Islander worth his salt has his own recipe for stuffies. Some are dripping with grease, some have hardly any clam. Robby goes out daily on his fishing vessel the "Sea Mule." His recipe makes spicy, clammy, pepper-packed stuffies, worthy of their name.

The Catch

9 4 inch Quahogs OR Surf Clams
½-¾ cups clam juice

The Groceries

1 pound ground chouriço
3 sleeves Ritz-style crackers
1 green pepper, chopped
1 red pepper, chopped
1 strong onion, chopped
3 stalks celery, chopped
1 jalapeño, chopped super fine
cooking spray

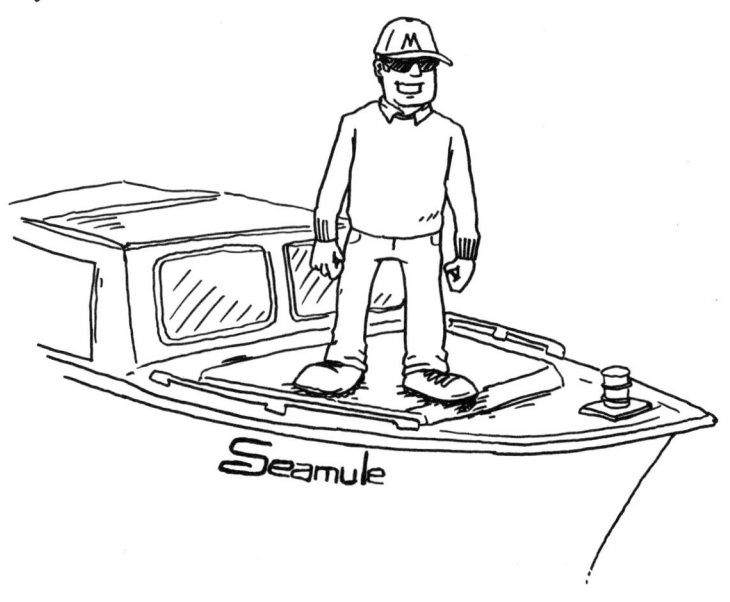

The How To

- FOLLOW directions for STEAMING BIG CLAMS FOR RE-COOKING (page 18). CLEAN meat as directed, CHOP roughly and set aside. SAVE and CLEAN the shells.
- BROWN chouriço in a frying pan over medium heat. If it is browning too much but not cooked through, add a little water and cook it off until the sausage is cooked and tender. RESIST the urge to pour off the oil! It has great flavor!
- CRUSH crackers into big crumbs. (A no-mess way is to put into a gallon-sized ziplock bag and smash.)
- COMBINE smushed crackers, chopped veggies, chouriço (with grease), and clams in your largest bowl.
- MIX with hands and ADD in enough clam juice so that the mixture will stick together enough to form a crumbly ball, but not so much that it turns gooey.
- SPRAY cooking spray on the inside of cleaned clam shells.
- STUFF shells generously, pressing firmly with your hands.
- BAKE at 325°F for 30 minutes then SPRAY tops with cooking spray so they will brown nicely and BAKE for 10 more minutes. (40 minutes total.)
- SERVE with chowdah!

Fisherman's Tip

You can freeze stuffies, but if so, don't cook first. Freeze them on a cookie sheet and then shove into a ziplock once frozen. They will be good for a few months.

Yield: 15-18 spicy stuffies.
Kitchen Time: Active 20 minutes. Bake 40 minutes.
In Season: Year-round.

Mushroom & Bacon Stuffies

A wonderful, hybrid of stuffies and stuffed mushrooms...plus bacon!

The Catch
6-8 3-4 inch Quahogs
OR 10-12 Cherrystones
OR 6-8 4-5 inch Surf Clams
(1 cup meat)

The Groceries
1 16-ounce package uncooked mushrooms, diced into ¼ inch pieces
4 slices bacon snipped into ½ inch pieces with scissors
4 cloves garlic, minced
1 stick butter, melted
1 cup fine breadcrumbs

The Gear
1 old wooden spoon or flat stick

The How To

- STEAM and CLEAN your clams according to STEAMING BIG CLAMS FOR RE-COOKING (page 18).
- CHOP, SNIP, MINCE, CRUMB, and MELT ingredients, respectively.
- MIX everything together in a big bowl.
- SPRAY the inside of your clean shells with cooking spray.
- PRESS the stuffing into the shells firmly. OIL your hands if the stuffing sticks to them.
- LAY the wooden spoon or stick in the middle of a cookie sheet. These stuffies like to 'spill their juice' as they naturally 'tip' down. PROP their droopy sides up on the wooden spoon so that their goodness won't spill.
- SLIDE cookie sheet into oven gently.
- BAKE at 400°F for 40 minutes or until top looks golden and crispy! Bacon will still be soft, but it will be fully cooked. (Insert a meat thermometer if you wish and make sure the internal temperature is over 165°F. Ours are usually at least 190°F.)

Fisherman's Tip

These stuffies are noisy while they cook, snapping, popping and crackling happily. Don't be alarmed...

Yield: 8 succulent stuffies.

Kitchen Time: Active 5 minutes. Bake 40 minutes.

In Season: Year-round.

Portuguese Littlenecks

- adapted from a recipe by the Brick Alley Pub's late Gary Mathias, printed in the 'Providence Journal' October 18, 2006, in a segment by Gail Ciampa titled "Portuguese Littlenecks." Copyright © 2012 The Providence Journal. Reproduced by permission.

Gary was a talented cook and an avid fisherman. This spicy, local appetizer is one of the many recipes that still has crowds flocking to 'the Brick.'

The Catch
32 Littlenecks, scrubbed

The Groceries
1 Tablespoon olive oil

1 pound chouriço links, sliced into ¼ inch medallions

2 large green peppers cut into ⅓ inch slices

2 onions, cut into ⅓ inch rings

2 cups clam juice

1 cup dry white wine

¼ teaspoon red pepper flakes (or more if the sausage is mild)

¾ cup fresh cilantro, chopped and divided

1 red bell pepper, minced

1 lemon cut into 8 wedges

The Extras
fresh crusty bread

The How To

- HEAT oil in large pot over medium-high heat.
- ADD chouriço and BROWN.
- ADD peppers and onion. SAUTÉ until vegetables are tender, stirring frequently.
- ADD clam juice, wine, and red pepper flakes. HEAT to a boil.
- REDUCE heat to medium. SIMMER 3 minutes.
- ADD Littlenecks. COVER and COOK until clams open, about 8 minutes. DISCARD any clams that do not open.
- STIR in ½ cup cilantro.
- TRANSFER mixture to large bowl.
- GARNISH with ¼ cup cilantro, red bell pepper and lemon wedges.
- SERVE with small bowls and fresh crusty bread.

Yield: Appetizer for 6.
Kitchen Time: 25 minutes.
In Season: Year-round.

Steamer Boil

-the Oliveira way

Steamed soft shell clams are one of those decadent, dip-in-butter tastes of summer. The keys are to get the sand out before cooking, AND steam them with their 'sides' so flavors share. Get the clams the night before or the morning of, so you'll have plenty of time to clean them.

The Catch

6 pounds soft shell clams (anywhere from 80-120 clams)

The Groceries

4 big potatoes, halved

4 onions, halved

1 pound chouriço links, cut into 2 inch lengths

2 Tablespoons garlic, chopped

1 teaspoon red pepper flakes

4 ears corn, shucked and cut into thirds

The Gear

cornmeal

cheesecloth to tie into bags

twine or twist-ties

lots of little bowls for butter and rinsing broth

non-iodized salt

The How To

To clean the sand out...

- DUMP the clams into a clean sink and cover with cold water.
- SWISH around for a minute or so. The water should get murky. DRAIN and rinse sand from the bottom of the sink. DO THIS three times.
- SPRINKLE a couple tablespoons of cornmeal and a couple tablespoons of non-iodized salt over the clams and FILL the sink back up. SWISH around and LET SIT 10 minutes. DRAIN and RINSE sand from sink. DO THIS four times – the fourth time with no cornmeal.
- SCRUB clams lightly and rinse well. If it isn't yet time for dinner, you can store clams in fridge for a few hours, dry, but covered by wet paper.

When clams are almost done soaking, or a ½ hour before dinner...

- GET out your biggest pot. ESTIMATE the amount of water it will take to cover potatoes, onions and chouriço, plus a little, and HEAT that much to a boil. COVER.
- ADD your potatoes, chouriço, onions, garlic and other seasonings. COVER and SIMMER.

Meanwhile...back to our clams...

- MAKE bags out of cheesecloth big enough to hold 10-12 steamers PLUS ½ as much room again (so they can open) and TIE with twine or twist-ties.
- TEST potatoes with a fork and when they are nearly done, ADD in <u>some</u> corn, and 5 minutes later, <u>some</u> clam bags. Steamers and corn are both best served hot – so it's best to have a rolling supply rather than to cook them all at once.
- LADLE cooking broth on top of clams and corn during cooking. Clams are done when they are fully open. REMOVE the clam bags and SCOOP some potatoes, onion, corn and chouriço onto a platter.
- MELT plenty of butter and put a little pot in front of each eater. LADLE some broth into small bowls for use as rinse water. INSTRUCT your eaters to discard any clams that aren't open.
- BEFORE you dig in, ADD more clam bags and corn to pot and CONTINUE to simmer remaining chouriço and onions. REPEAT until everyone's full!

Yield: Dinner for 6-8.

Kitchen Time: Soaking clams 1+ hours. 'Boil' 45-ish minutes.

Season: Summertime, when the livin' is easy...

Steaming Big Clams for Re-Cooking

A lot of recipes call for 'a cup of chopped clams.' It's usually better to have these clams undercooked — so they won't be tough in your final dish after you cook them again. These directions apply to 'Big Clams' (Quahogs and Surf Clams). Steamers are a whole different kettle of fish and get their own directions in the 'Steamer Boil.' (page 16)

The Catch
hard shell clams

Clam Math

8 3 inch Quahogs
    yield 1 cup meat

6 4 inch Quahogs
    yield 1 cup meat

8 4 inch Surf Clams
    yield 1 cup meat

6 5 inch Surf Clams
    yield 1 cup meat

The How To

Steaming to just open...

- BOIL an inch of water in a big pot with a steamer basket.
- Once boiling, ADD the big clams, COVER, and STEAM until they are mostly slightly open. (Probably less than ten minutes)
- REMOVE the 'open' ones into a big bowl. Give any 'hold outs' two more minutes. If they still aren't open – DISCARD. The 'hold outs' tend to be the most sandy!
- SHUCK clams over the clam bowl so more juice can be collected. USE a dull knife to get as much of the clam as you can out of the shell. SET ASIDE the clam meat, and POUR any bowl juice into the pot.

> *Fisherman's Tip:* Getting all the sand out of your clams is the difference between an amazing meal and a chipped tooth.

Cleaning the sand out ...

- Over the sink, PICK UP the meat of one cooked clam. It will easily come apart into two sections. One hand will hold the 'foot' (triangular tongue looking part) and the belly filled with flavorful brown mushy stuff. RINSE any sand off this part and put in a clean bowl, including the brown mushy stuff!
- The other hand will hold the mantle ('lips') and the dark siphon or 'tube' of the clam. Sand is lurking in this part! RINSE any you see, and be sure to BREAK OPEN the 'tube' as sand absolutely hides in there. Feeling lazy? – just SNIP the 'tubes' off.
- CHOP up the clams and REFRIGERATE until you're ready to make your recipe.

Remembering the juice...

- POUR your clam juice into a tall cylinder. (A 'take-out' soup container works okay.)
- LET it sit for at least 5 minutes so sand falls to the bottom.
- POUR all but the last inch of juice through a coffee filter or paper towel, TWICE.
- REFRIGERATE for up to 4 days or FREEZE for up to 3 months.

Yield: Partially cooked clams. For volume see "Clam Math" on left.

Kitchen Time: Cook 10 minutes.

Cleaning and shucking 5 minutes per dozen clams.

In Season: Year-round.

White Clam Pizza

If you look up recipes for clam pizza on the internet, 100 percent of them miss the boat. They have clams on the pizza, but their briny richness is <u>absent from the sauce</u>...which makes the clams seem strangely out of place. Finally, a pie for the clam lover!

The Catch

6-8 3-4 inch Quahogs
OR 10-12 Cherrystones
OR 6-8 4-5 inch Surf Clams
   (1 cup meat)
¾ cup clam juice

The Groceries

4 teaspoons lemon juice
3 Tablespoons flour
½ cup sour cream
8 cloves garlic, finely
   chopped, divided
pizza dough
1 teaspoon olive oil
1 teaspoon fresh rosemary,
   minced
2 cups shredded mozzarella
   cheese
2 slices bacon, snipped into
   1 inch pieces

The How To

- STEAM, and CLEAN your clams according to STEAMING BIG CLAMS FOR RE-COOKING (page 18).
- PRE-HEAT oven to 400°F (or temperature on pizza dough package).
- MAKE a 'slurry' with cooled clam juice, lemon juice and flour by WHISKING them together in a cool saucepan.
- THICKEN over high heat until whisk lines stay visible, STIRRING to prevent lumps and browning.
- REMOVE from heat, STIR in sour cream and 4 cloves worth of minced garlic.
- STRETCH pizza dough onto greased cookie sheet or heated pizza stone.
- SMEAR 'white sauce' on dough – leaving an inch at the edges blank.
- SPRINKLE clams and rosemary evenly.
- SPRINKLE cheese evenly.
- MIX remaining garlic with 1 teaspoon olive oil. SPRINKLE on top. DISTRIBUTE bacon pieces evenly so no one feels left out.
- COOK at 400°F until cheese is golden brown, bacon looks cooked, and you simply can't stand it any longer. (At least 20 minutes.)
- COOL at least five minutes if you value the roof of your mouth...
- SLICE and ENJOY!

Yield: Dinner for 4.
Kitchen Time: Active 20 minutes. Bake 20-30 minutes.
In Season: Year-round.

About Conch...

Surprise – Rhode Island's waters are filled with conch! Unlike flashier lobster and Striped Bass, conch doesn't get much room on local restaurant menus. This could be due to the time it takes to cook (a bunch) or because they have only recently begun to be commercially fished. Local conch is important in Italian cooking (known as 'scungilli') and in Asian culture served raw. It is a chewy, lean meat, similar to the foot of a clam but completely sand free!

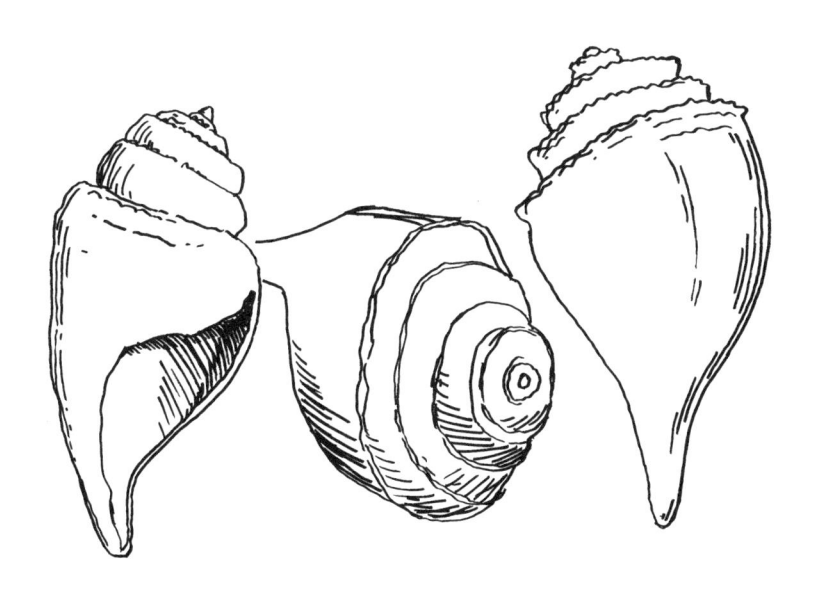

The Local Catch

The 'conch' caught around Aquidneck Island aren't actually conch. Their true name is *'channel whelk' (Busycotypus canaliculatus)* but everyone calls them conch. True conch or "Queen Conch" are vegetarians and live in warmer waters (think Bahamas and pink shells...). Our 'conch' are gray carnivorous little suckers. They live along the bottom of the ocean and show up in lobster traps all the time. Commercial conch fishing requires a license endorsement while RI residents are allowed to catch one half bushel per day. Conch is sold live at local markets or frozen labeled 'scungilli.'

Which is which?

You don't need to be able to tell conch apart as local conch are mostly one species, but you do need to know 'which part' is edible. You only want the 'white' part. The gray digestive track is NOT desirable and is the source of an unpleasant smell while cooking. In all our recipes we are banking on the fact that you've already cut out the bad stuff and harvested only the 'white' meat. Here are three ways to get the conch out of the shell so you can trim it to just the part you want:

1. Smash with hammer and trim while still on the boat or outside.
Kitchen mess and smell = none.

2. Freeze for two hours and then hang from a fish hook stuck into the meat. The shell will fall right off and you can cut out the bad parts.
Kitchen mess and smell = minimal.

3. Cook for ten minutes then pull out of shell.
Kitchen mess and smell = ferocious.

We suggest method 1 or 2.

Conch 'Math'

1 *pound* of conch in-shell yields just under ½ pound uncooked meat

2 *Conch* yield 1 cup uncooked meat or ¾ cup cooked meat

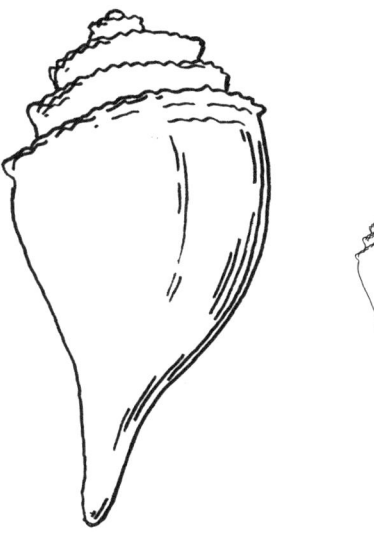

Kitchen Must:

Cook it until it's tender.

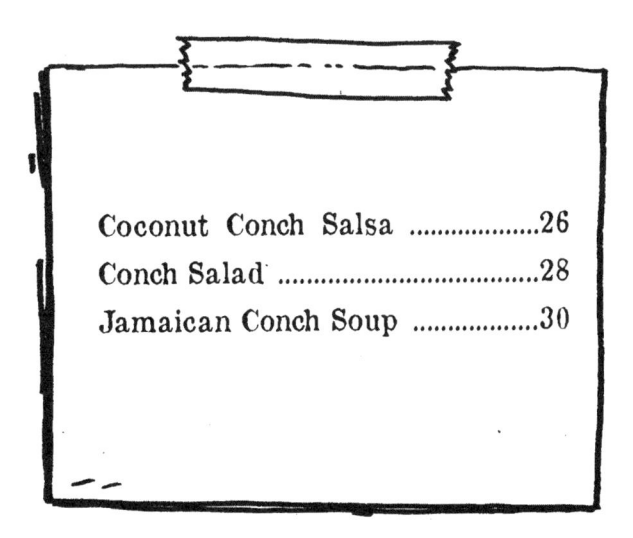

Coconut Conch Salsa	26
Conch Salad	28
Jamaican Conch Soup	30

Coconut Conch Salsa

Local conch is chewy and absorbs flavors well. Add a little 'local' to your homemade salsa to sneak in some lean protein.

The Catch
4 conch

The Groceries
2 Tablespoons lemon juice
2 teaspoons baking soda
1 cup coconut milk
juice of 1 lime with pulp
juice of 1 small orange with pulp
1 teaspoon hot sauce
1 cup grape tomatoes, quartered
½ red onion, chopped fine
¼ cup red pepper, chopped
½ cup cilantro or parsley, chopped

The Extras
tortilla chips

The How To

- START with conch that have been broken from the shell, dark parts removed and only 'white meat' remaining (page 24).
- QUARTER conch meat.
- RINSE in bowl with 2 tablespoons lemon juice and some water for one minute.
- BOIL conch meat in a half-filled pot with baking soda for 1 hour. SKIM foam or it makes a mess.
- DICE conch meat into ¼ inch cubes.
- COMBINE all ingredients in a non-reactive bowl, taking care to include as much of the 'pulp' as you can from the citrus.
- LET SIT at least 6 hours in the fridge, mixing occasionally. If you are letting it sit for longer, you might need to add more fresh tomatoes before serving.
- DRAIN the juice.
- SERVE with tortilla chips.

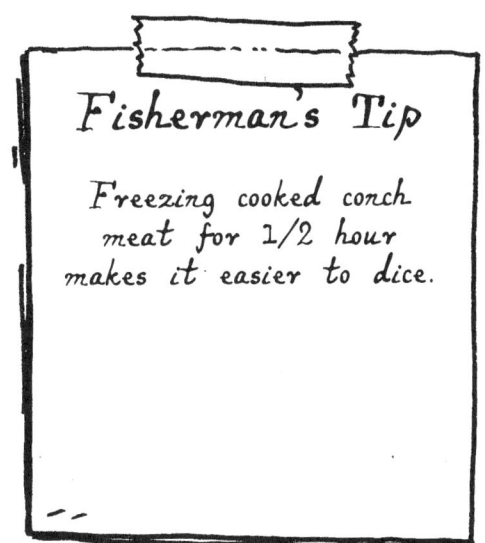

Fisherman's Tip

Freezing cooked conch meat for 1/2 hour makes it easier to dice.

Yield: 4 cups of salsa.

Kitchen Time: Active 10 minutes. Simmer 1 hour. Marinate 6 hours.

In Season: Year-round.

Conch Salad

— Denny's way

The key to perfect conch is cooking it until it's tender, then slicing it wafer thin. Then you've got a lean, pleasantly chewy, totally unique side salad that will be the talk of your seafood barbeque. Pick a day when you're puttering around the house as it takes a little effort... and a <u>lot</u> of time.

The Catch

10 conch

The Groceries

- ¼ cup baking soda
- 1 large red onion, chopped
- 2 stalks celery, chopped
- 1 small can sliced black olives (2-4 ounces)
- 8 ounces yellow 'hot pepper rings' and juice from jar
- 1 Tablespoon oregano
- 1 16-ounce bottle of Italian dressing, or equivalent balsamic vinegar and olive oil

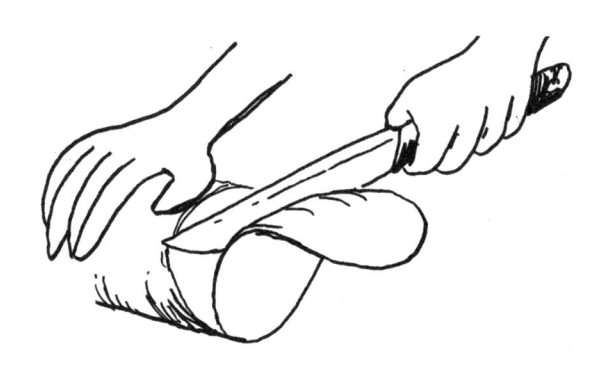

The How To

- START with conch that have been broken from the shell, dark parts removed and only 'white meat' remaining (page 24).
- FILL your biggest pot halfway and bring to a boil.
- ADD conch meat and baking soda.
- RETURN water to a boil then ADJUST heat so it is simmering just below a 'rolling boil.'
- SKIM the foam off the top. (The foaming will stop after about 20 minutes and skimming cuts down on the mess.)
- SIMMER like this for 90 minutes or a little longer, until meat is tender and fork goes in easily.
- DRAIN water and cool conch 15 minutes.
- FREEZE conch for 1 hour so it will be easy to slice.
- SLICE conch into wafer thin pieces using a meat slicer OR a steak knife and patience.
- COMBINE conch wafers, chopped onion, celery, olives, hot pepper rings with juice, oregano, AND bottle of Italian dressing OR equivalent balsamic vinegar and olive oil.
- REFRIGERATE overnight, stirring a few times.
- TASTE it and decide what else it 'needs,' (salt, pepper, bell peppers, herbs, hot sauce.) and ADD.
- SERVE cold as a unique, healthy side salad!

Fisherman's Tip: As it takes hours to cook conch meat- we do it in one big batch and then freeze extra meat for up to three months. Vacuum sealers are great.

Yield: 8 cups of side salad.
Kitchen Time: Active 25 minutes. Simmer 90 minutes. Marinate overnight.
In Season: Year-round.

Jamaican Conch Soup

– Ronnie's way

The island has a significant Jamaican community and they're known for their spicy conch soup. The earthy 'ocean' taste of the conch is complemented by the root veggies. It's a simple recipe, but requires a whole 'day you don't mind chillin.' Making the dumplings is a great job for kids!

The Catch
6 conch

The Groceries
½ cup lemon juice

salt

2 'Scotch Bonnet' hot peppers

3 sprigs fresh thyme

4 carrots, peeled and diced

3 potatoes, peeled and diced

1 cup yucca, peeled and diced

3 scallions, bruised and halved

¾ cup okra, chopped

3 packets 'Cock' brand spicy soup mix (found in the Jamaican section of Stop & Shop)

4 cups flour

The Gear
<u>loud</u> reggae music

The How To

- START with conch that have been broken from the shell, dark parts removed and only 'white meat' remaining (page 24).
- WASH conch meat in a bowl filled with enough water to cover conch, plus ½ cup lemon juice, wiping off anything that will come off.
- CHOP conch into ¼-½ inch pieces.
- BOIL water in a stockpot filled halfway. When boiling, ADD teaspoon salt and conch meat.
- BOIL for 90 minutes, ADDING additional ingredients at the listed times. SKIM foam as it forms, being careful not to skim off conch pieces. Meanwhile, MAKE DUMPLINGS as described below.
- At 30 minutes, PIERCE one 'Scotch Bonnet' pepper and ADD to pot with thyme.
- At 45 minutes, ADD dumplings. ADD water as needed so there is about 6 inches of water above the conch meat.
- At 60 minutes, ADD potatoes, yucca, carrots, and remaining 'Scotch Bonnet,' pierced.
- At 70 minutes, ADD okra, scallions and 3 packets soup mix.
- At 80 minutes, ADJUST spice by adding soup mix or water.
- At 90 minutes, SERVE and ENJOY! Make sure to SCOOP the conch meat from the bottom.

To make dumplings:

- MIX 4 cups flour and ½ teaspoon salt with 1 cup water in a large bowl.
- KNEAD dough with your hands while gradually ADDING approximately 1 more cup water. The amount of water depends on humidity and lots of factors, but you are aiming for a dough that is wet enough to hold all the flour together, but not so wet as to be sticky.
- KNEAD until dough is consistent. When you pinch it, it should 'spring' back.
- BREAK dough into 2 inch balls and HAND ROLL into ½ inch thick dumplings, any shape...pancakes, baby carrot shape, whatever. This is a great job for kids.
- DROP into soup at appropriate time.

Yield: Dinner for 6-8.
Kitchen Time: Between 90 minutes and 2 hours.
In Season: Year-round.

About Crabs...

Crab may very well be Rhode Island's unsung seafood treasure. Cranky and plentiful, these crustaceans scuttle sideways around the ocean floor year-round, sneaking in and out of lobster traps for free snacks. You must work for your crab dinner as there is no good alternative to hand-picking their sweet meat. However, local crab is well worth the effort, delicious on its own, as well as in stuffings, soups and chowders.

The Local Catch

Local crabs aren't 'Deadliest Catch' huge. They tend to be between 4-7 inches wide yielding about ¼ cup+ meat each, depending on whether or not you are an experienced 'picker.' Sand Crabs, Rock Crabs and Blue Crabs are all edible and reside locally. Though Sand and Rock Crabs are so plentiful there is no commercial 'limit' on them, Blue Crabs do not exist in significant numbers and are not fished commercially at all. Rhode Island residents may catch certain crabs recreationally with no license.

Which is which?

Welcome to Rhode Island where we sometimes make up our own names for things. For instance, there actually is no state named Rhode Island. Surprise! The state you think of as Rhode Island is actually named, 'The State of Rhode Island and Providence Plantations.' Similarly, the island we refer to as 'Aquidneck Island' is truly named 'Rhode Island,' just to keep things interesting... We are no less creative when referring to seafood.

There are two kinds of crabs widely eaten locally: 'Rock Crabs,' (their true name being Jonah Crabs) and 'Sand Crabs' (their true name being Rock Crabs). No kidding. 'Rock Crabs' live near rock. 'Sand Crabs' live near sand...and so that's what the fishermen call them. The RI Department of Environmental Management's 'Official Species Codes' even acknowledge the trend: CRJ = Crab, Jonah (Rock Crab); CRR = Crab, Rock (Sand Crab). No need to worry that you might be mis-served at the fish market. Just forget you read this and use the nicknames that have completely taken over the Ocean State. No doubt the world will someday catch up with our ingenuity.

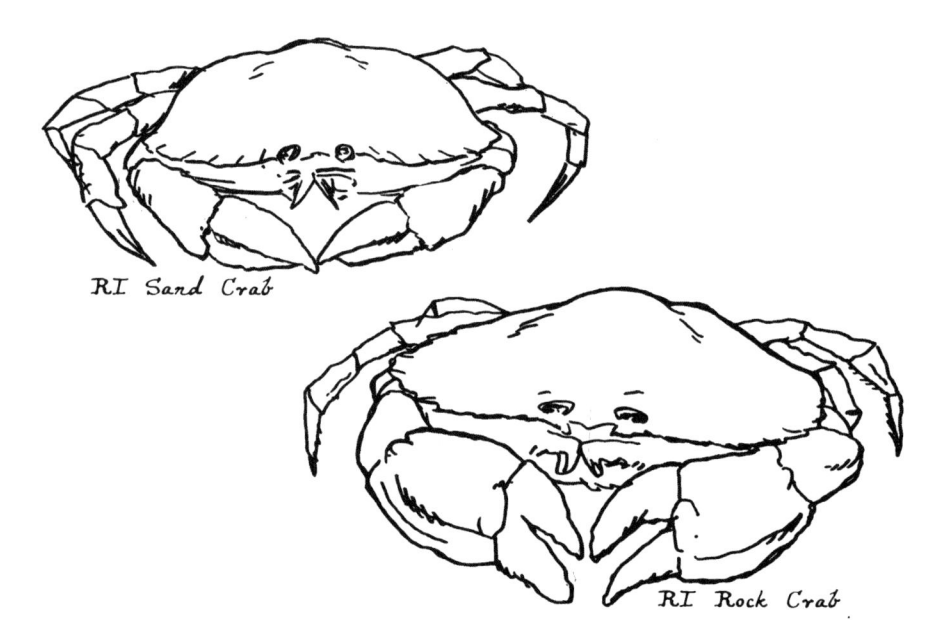

RI Sand Crab

RI Rock Crab

RI Sand Crabs *(Cancer irroratus)* have coveted sweet meat and smaller claws than their rocky brothers. They are generally no more than 5 inches wide at the carapace (body). On each side of the eyes, there are nine vestigial 'teeth' or bumps at the edge of the shell. (See illustration, left.) They are primarily a 'bay' or 'in-shore' catch.

RI Rock Crabs *(Cancer borealis)* have meat that is a little less sweet than their sandy brothers, but their claws are big, making for easy picking. They can grow to be larger than 8 inches wide and prefer deeper water. The carapace edge to either side of the eyes is smooth, distinguishing it from a 'Sand' crab. (See illustration, left.) Many summer in-shore lobstermen fish these 'Jonah crabs' off-shore in winter.

Crab 'Math'

4   5 inch Sand Crabs
       yield 1 cup meat.

3   5 inch Rock Crabs
       yield 1 cup meat.

Kitchen Must:

Don't forget the meat in the bodies!

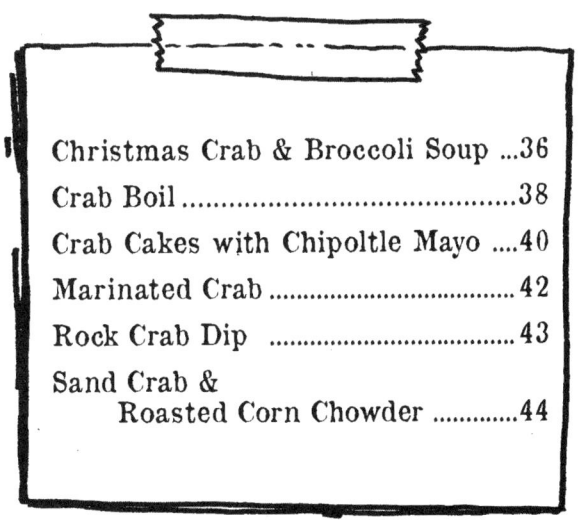

Christmas Crab & Broccoli Soup	36
Crab Boil	38
Crab Cakes with Chipoltle Mayo	40
Marinated Crab	42
Rock Crab Dip	43
Sand Crab & Roasted Corn Chowder	44

Christmas Crab & Broccoli Soup

– Dave Spencer's way

This simple, hearty soup is a staple at the Spencer Christmas holidays, ensuring that Dave graces the kitchen at least once a year. Tons of 'red' crab meat and green broccoli combine to make a 'festive' holiday soup, tasty in any season.

The Catch

16 crabs, steamed (page 38) and picked
(2 pounds meat)

The Groceries

2 pounds fresh broccoli
½ stick butter
1 medium onion, chopped
4 Tablespoons flour
3 cups half & half
3 cups milk
2 chicken bouillon cubes
½ teaspoon black pepper
½ teaspoon cayenne pepper
1 teaspoon dried thyme
1 teaspoon paprika
more paprika for garnish

The How To

- CHOP broccoli florets into 1 inch pieces, and stems into ½ inch pieces.
- MELT butter in large pot over medium heat.
- SOFTEN chopped onions until translucent.
- STIR in flour to form a 'roux' of peanut butter consistency.
- WHISK in milk and half & half and SIMMER about 7 minutes, STIRRING until texture changes slightly. (This is not a thick broth.)
- DISSOLVE bouillon cubes in soup. ADD spices.
- ADD broccoli and RETURN to simmer.
- SIMMER 5 minutes and ADD crab.
- SIMMER until broccoli is just cooked. It should still be firm and be bright green.
- SERVE with a sprinkle of paprika!

Fisherman's Tip

This soup doesn't have a lot of 'liquid' in it and it loses some during re-heating. Add some milk when re-heating to 'juice' it back up.

Yield: Dinner for 5 or 10 cups of hearty soup.
Kitchen Time: 40 minutes.
In Season: Year-round.

Crab Boil*

— Russell's way

In summer, an island picnic table simply begs for a hungry crowd and a pile of steamed crabs. Get your crew, a few beverages, and pick the sweet meat out of these local crustaceans. Local Rock and Sand Crabs are about 5 inches across. If yours are larger — steam them longer!

*Crab 'Boil' is just a name. <u>Steam</u> your crabs.

The Catch
dozen Sand or Rock Crabs per batch

The Groceries
1 beer
Old Bay seasoning

The Extras
corn on the cob
melted butter

The Gear
'pickers' like metal toothpicks or plastic forks with one tine

The How To

- BOIL 1 inch of water and 1 beer in the biggest pot you have, with a steamer basket.
- DROP in a few crabs. SPRINKLE in some Old Bay seasoning.
- DROP in some more crabs. SPRINKLE more Old Bay seasoning.
- CONTINUE until all your crabs are in and COVER with a tight lid.
- STEAM for 12-15 minutes until they are all bright bright red.
- PLUNGE in ice water immediately.
- REMOVE quickly and SERVE!
- DON'T FORGET, there's meat in the body – not just the legs!

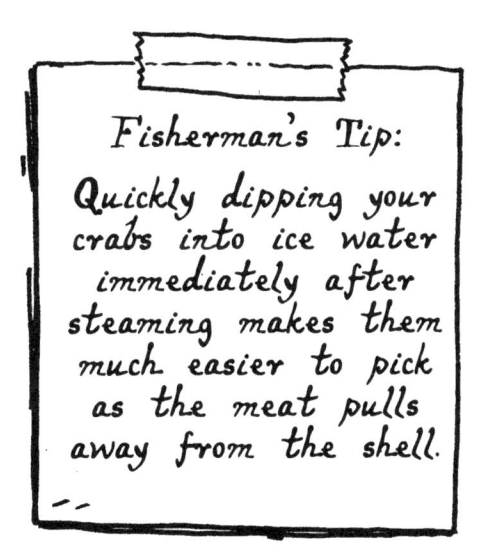

Fisherman's Tip: Quickly dipping your crabs into ice water immediately after steaming makes them much easier to pick as the meat pulls away from the shell.

Yield: Estimate 5-7 crabs per eater for dinner.

Kitchen Time: 15 minutes.

Season: Year-round.

Crab Cakes with Chipotle Mayo

This is a great way to enjoy crab and kids love to 'draw' with the mayo. Cakes can be frozen for an easy dinner down the line!

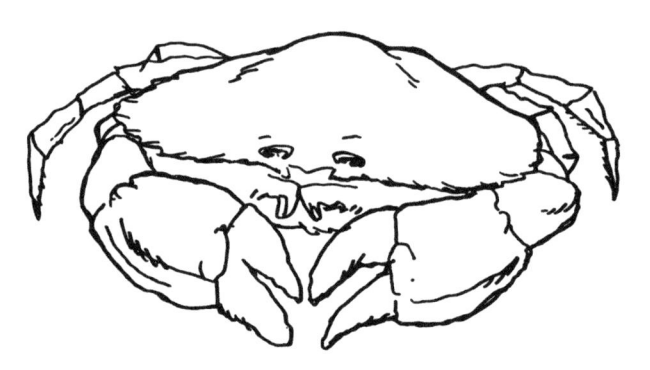

The Catch

8 crabs, steamed (page 38) and picked
(1 pound meat)

The Groceries

1 cup mayonnaise, divided
1 teaspoon chipotle pepper 'adobo' sauce (comes in a small can in the Spanish section)
1 8½-ounce can of corn (about 1 cup)
2 sleeves Ritz-style crackers
1 teaspoon Old Bay seasoning
½ cup chopped scallions
butter

The Extras

salad greens in light dressing

The How To

To prepare chipotle mayonnaise...

- MIX ½ cup mayonnaise and 1 teaspoon chipotle 'adobo' sauce in a small ziplock bag. REFRIGERATE. When ready to garnish, SNIP small hole in bottom corner of bag and SQUEEZE mayo out as if in a pastry tube.

To prepare crab cakes...

- CRUSH crackers into big crumbs. (A no-mess way is to put into a gallon-sized ziplock bag and smash.)
- PRESS moisture out of crab meat with a paper towel.
- DRAIN corn and DRY on a paper towel.
- COMBINE cracker crumbs, corn, crab meat, scallions, ½ cup mayo and teaspoon Old Bay in big bowl.
- MIX with your hands.
- FORM into patties approximately 1 inch thick and 3-4 inches in diameter.
- PUT some flour on a plate and PAT each cake into flour before cooking. This will help each form a crust.
- MELT a few tablespoons of butter in a skillet over medium heat.
- FRY each cake in butter, 3 minutes each side. The less you move them around, the easier a crust will form. REPLENISH butter when pan dries out.
- SERVE crab cakes on a bed of dressed salad greens.
- DRAW fun designs on each cake with chipotle mayo. ENJOY!

Yield: Dinner for 8 or 10-12 cakes.
Kitchen Time: 25 minutes, plus picking crab.
In Season: Year-round.

Marinated Crab

- Denny's way

A great way to enjoy crabs 'later.' The dressing's flavors seep into the crab meat for a nice change.

The Catch
dozen crabs

The Groceries
1 'big' bottle Italian dressing (16 ounces)

The Extras
'pickers' like metal toothpicks or plastic forks with one tine

The How To
- STEAM your crabs in an inch of water for 12-15 minutes until bright red.
- DIP in ice-water immediately.
- CHOP crabs in half, down the center. RINSE out the 'guts.'
- MIX crab bodies and dressing together in non-reactive bowl. REFRIGERATE overnight, MIXING a few times.
- PICK and EAT cold crabs as usual and enjoy the 'different' taste!

Yield: Appetizer for 6.
Kitchen Time: Prep 5 minutes, plus picking crab. Marinate overnight.
In Season: Year-round.

Rock Crab Dip

- Chris' way

The Rock Crab's big claws make the picking easy and the crowd happy.

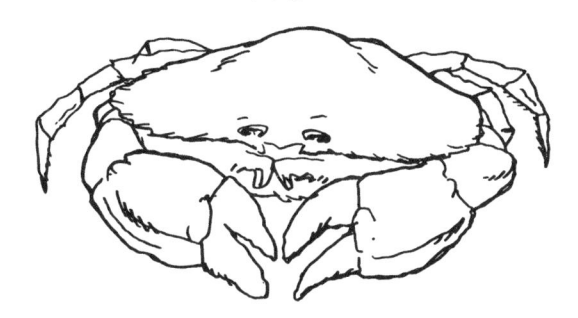

The Catch
8 Rock Crabs, steamed (page 38) and picked (1 pound meat)

The Groceries
2 8-ounce packages chive cream cheese
1 medium onion, diced
¼ cup mayonnaise
2 Tablespoons horseradish
2 Tablespoons ketchup

The Extras
a 'bread bowl' to serve in
chips or veggies to dip with

The How To
- MIX all but crab meat with a mixer to get it smooth.
- STIR in crab meat.
- TASTE. ADJUST seasonings. SERVE.

Yield: Appetizer.
Kitchen Time: 5 minutes, plus picking crab.
In Season: Year-round.

Sand Crab & Roasted Corn Chowder

by Bill Solitro

Bill is known at the pier for this rich chowder. It requires a fair bit of work: roasting corn, baking potatoes, and hand-picking crab, but the crave-able sweet, spicy, smoky, crabby, creamy flavor (and the praise that comes from your eaters) makes the time fly!

The Catch

6 Sand Crabs

The Groceries

6 medium red potatoes

6 ears corn

5 Tablespoons butter

4 strips bacon

4 stalks celery, diced

2 medium onions, diced

4 carrots, diced

3 Tablespoons flour

black pepper

1 teaspoon red pepper flakes

½ teaspoon garlic powder

2-3 cups heavy cream

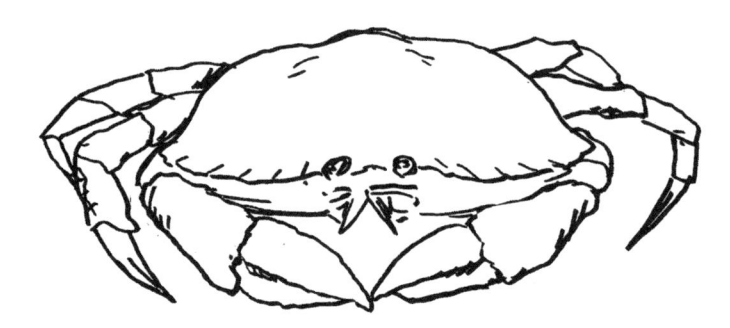

The How To

- BAKE potatoes. PEEL and DICE.
- ROAST ears of corn and slice kernels off. You want some kernels to be slightly black as that's what gives the chowder its smoky flavor.
- BOIL 1 gallon water in your biggest pot. DROP in Sand Crabs and simmer for 15 minutes.
- SAVE the water.
- PLUNGE each crab in ice water briefly.
- PICK the crabs, remembering the bodies contain a bunch of meat. SET ASIDE meat.
- SNIP bacon into ½ inch pieces over another big pot.
- BROWN over medium heat.
- ADD in butter, diced celery, onion and carrot. COOK until vegetables start getting soft.
- STIR in flour to make a 'roux' of a peanut butter consistency.
- STIR in red pepper flakes, garlic powder, black pepper, heavy cream and 2 to 3 cups of the crabs' steaming water.
- HEAT to a simmer.
- ADD roasted corn kernels and diced baked potatoes.
- STIR in crab meat and SERVE.

> **Fisherman's Tip**
>
> To 'roast' ears of corn quickly, turn on the stove and hold corn against a burner until it starts to brown.

Yield: A pot of the best darn chowder you'll ever taste.
Kitchen Time: Lots.
In Season: Year-round.

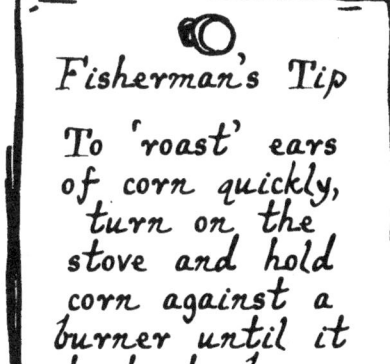

About Fish...

It should come as no surprise that the 'Ocean State' is home to a few fish... Rhode Island's craggy ports, harbors and bays make for some of the best fishing in New England. Its seaside towns are renowned for their seafood restaurants, though, strangely most of the fish served in them is caught nowhere near here. Delicious Sea Bass, Flounder, Blackfish and Cod swim laps around the island while popular 'Chilean' Sea Bass, Tilapia and Salmon arrive frozen via plane. Fresh caught fish is delicious. Less fresh fish is less delicious. Local fish is the freshest and therefore the delicious-est.

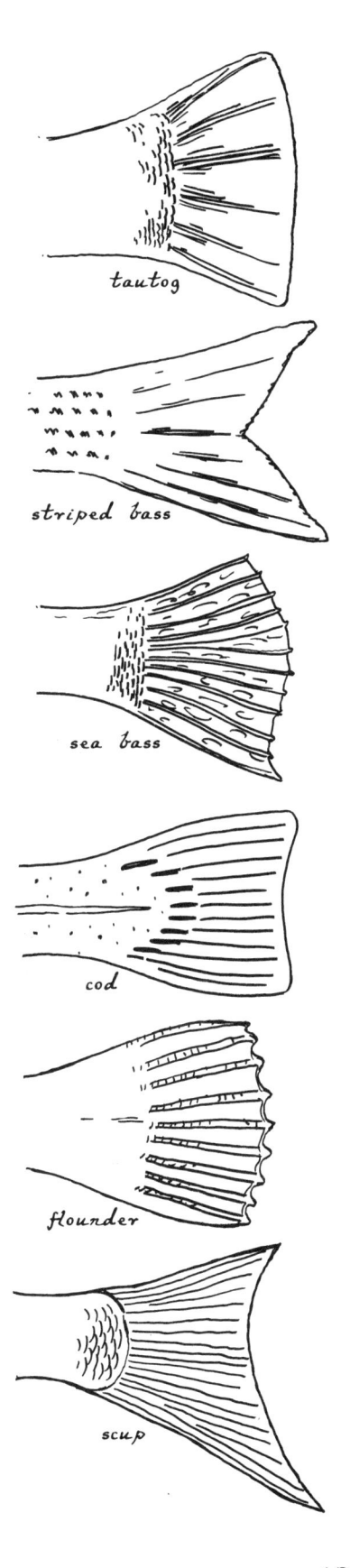

tautog

striped bass

sea bass

cod

flounder

scup

The Local Catch

Rhode Island's waters are home to countless varieties of 'swimming' fish. They are caught in big boats, and little boats, from standing on shore and by anchoring off. Hooks, nets, spears, draggers and traps are all used locally to land them. All saltwater fishing in the state of Rhode Island requires some type of license.

Fishing licensing requirements, seasonal openings, species limits, etc, require years of experience and/or a college degree to understand. All you really need to know is that you need to know. Fishery laws, limits, licenses and protections exist so that our children's children can get the chance to enjoy the taste of wild caught fish. *Fish responsibly.*

Which is which?

With the exception of Bluefish, almost all the fish caught locally have flaky white meat. Blackfish (Tautog), Striped Bass, Cod and Black Sea Bass are 'thick,' while Flounder and Scup are relatively 'thin.' Monkfish requires its own category as it is 'triangle' shaped. Pretty much any local fish can be baked, fried, grilled, sautéed, put into chowder, etc – though there are some stereotypical ways to eat each.

Tautog, or Blackfish, is a thick, firm fleshed fish that holds up great in soup and chowder. It freezes really well.

Black Sea Bass, according to Denny Ingram, is "the flakiest, sweetest, fish out there." It is interchangeable with the more well known *Cod*.

Striped Bass and **Scup** are great to grill skin-on as their skin tends to hold up and they do well with the smoky flavor.

Flounder is thin and does well pan-fried.

Monkfish sports a unique triangle shape and a firm, lobster-like texture. Only the tails are used in most cooking. It holds up well in grilled kabobs and stir-fry.

Bluefish can be tricky. If not eaten 'the day of', it can become unpleasantly fishy. However, as a smoked fish, it is worth its weight in gold. Visit www.FishermansTable.com to watch a video on how to smoke a Bluefish!

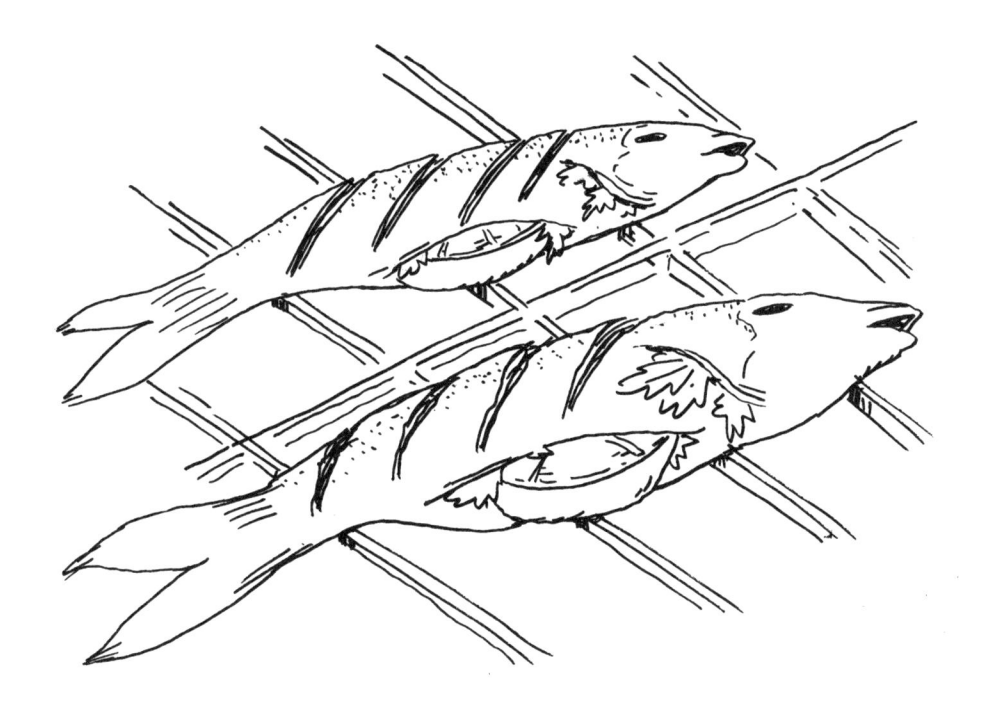

Fish 'Math'

Estimate 1 pound fish fillet per person for dinner. Less if served with lots of 'extras.'

Kitchen Must:

Fish must be fresh.

Blackfish Cioppino	50
Fast Baked Fish, Potato and Vegetable	52
Fish Stock	54
Fish Tacos	56
Flounder Francese	58
Grilled Whole Fish	60
Portuguese Baked Blackfish	62
Portuguese Fish Chowder	64
Sweet & Sour Monkfish Stir-Fry	66
Sweet Potato Fish Cakes	68

Blackfish Cioppino

Blackfish's firm texture makes it great in soups. This simple tomato-based fish soup begs for a rainy day and fresh bread.
Use homemade stock in the recipe to get the most out of your fish. It is even better the second day after the flavors share!

The Catch
1 ½ pounds Blackfish (Tautog) fillets

The Groceries
1 Tablespoon olive oil

1 small onion, chopped

1 medium carrot, chopped

3 cloves garlic, chopped

½ teaspoon red pepper flakes

1 8-ounce can tomato sauce

1 28-ounce can crushed tomatoes

1 bay leaf

4 cups FISH STOCK (page 54) OR clam juice

1 teaspoon dried basil

1 teaspoon dried thyme

1 teaspoon dried marjoram

¼ teaspoon saffron (optional)

1 cup dry white wine

1 Tablespoon fresh parsley, chopped fine

black pepper

The Extras
fresh crusty bread

The How To

- HEAT olive oil in big stock pot over medium-high heat.
- SOFTEN onion, carrot and garlic until tender – without burning garlic.
- ADD tomato sauce, tomatoes, white wine, fish stock and all seasonings except parsley.
- SIMMER for one hour, stirring occasionally.
- CUT fish into 'bite-sized' pieces.
- ADD fish and SIMMER for 10 minutes.
- SERVE sprinkled with black pepper and chopped parsley.

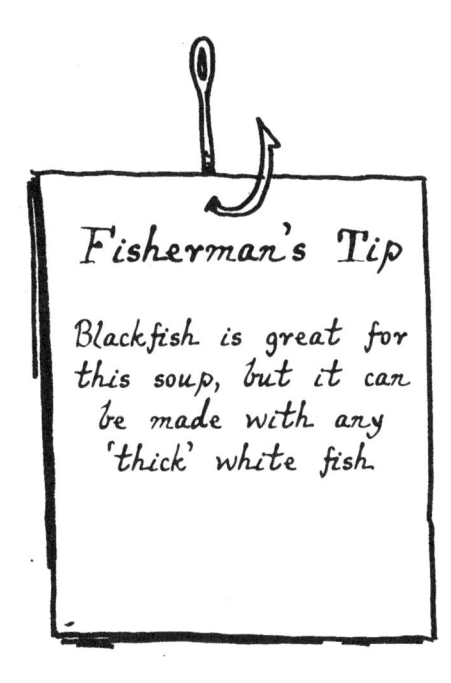

Fisherman's Tip

Blackfish is great for this soup, but it can be made with any 'thick' white fish.

Yield: 4 bowls or 7 cups.

Kitchen Time: Active 15 minutes. Simmer 70 minutes.

In Season: April to December.

Fast Baked Fish, Potato, & Vegetable

'Plan A' for dinner when you come home with fish and are starving.

The Catch

fresh 'white' fish fillets at least 1 inch thick (estimate 1 pound per eater)

The Groceries

1 medium potato per eater

1 lemon, wedged

dried dill

pepper

fresh asparagus or green beans

½ cup milk

salt

cooking spray

1 Tablespoon butter **per fillet**

2 Tablespoons breadcrumbs from the cardboard tube **per fillet**

The How To

- SET the oven to 550°F.
- POKE potatoes with fork four times each. WRAP each in a moist paper towel. MICROWAVE for 3½ minutes times the number of potatoes.
- GREASE with cooking spray both a baking dish (for fish) and a cookie sheet (for vegetable.)
- WASH asparagus or beans and TRIM ends.
- SPREAD vegetables on cookie sheet and SPRAY top with cooking spray. This will help them brown slightly. SPRINKLE with salt if you like.
- MELT 1 tablespoon butter per fillet in a small dish. MIX with 2 tablespoons breadcrumbs per fillet.
- WASH and DRY your fish fillets.
- SALT a small bowl of milk. DIP each fillet in salted milk. SHAKE.
- ARRANGE on baking dish. SPRINKLE with lemon, dill, and pepper. COVER fillets with breadcrumbs.
- SET timer for 10 minutes and slide fish onto top rack of oven.
- AFTER 4 minutes, SLIDE vegetable cookie sheet onto lower rack of oven. RUB oil or spray cooking spray on unwrapped potatoes. PLACE potatoes directly on oven rack. COOK 6 minutes, giving fish 10 minutes total.
- CHECK and REMOVE if done. Vegetables should be bright green and still slightly firm. Fish should be opaque and flake easily with a fork. Breadcrumbs should be brown. If fish needs a little more time, shut off oven and fish will stop browning but finish cooking. Check with fork every 2 additional minutes.
- SQUEEZE lemon over both fish and veggies and SERVE. You have made a well rounded dinner in 20 minutes!

Fisherman's Tip: If you line the baking dish with tinfoil there is basically no clean up from this fast meal.

Yield: For dinner, estimate 1 pound fish per eater, 1 potato and some veggies.
Kitchen Time: 20 minutes.
In Season: Year-round.

Fish Stock

"You can make a whole lot of something out of nothing." Home-made fish-stock is basically free and a million times better than anything you can purchase.

The Catch
fish carcass (head, bones, skin, tail, everything, of any white fish)

The Groceries
4 Tablespoons olive oil
2 stalks celery, chopped (1 cup)
2 onions, chopped (2 cups)
2 carrots, chopped (1 cup)
2 cloves garlic, chopped
1 cup white wine
5 parsley stems OR
   ¼ teaspoon dried
pinch fresh thyme OR
   ¼ teaspoon dried
5 peppercorns
1 bay leaf

The Gear
cheesecloth

The How To

- HEAT oil in your biggest pot on medium.
- ADD the celery, carrots and onion. SOFTEN for about 5 minutes.
- ADD fish carcass. COOK for 1 minute.
- ADD garlic. COOK for 1 minute.
- DEGLAZE pot with wine using the wine to loosen any browned bits stuck to pan bottom and sides. Let it BURN OFF for a minute or two.
- POUR in enough water to cover everything by one or two inches.
- ADD spices.
- BOIL then reduce heat to SIMMER for 90 minutes. Stock may 'foam.' SKIM off foam if you are so inclined.
- STRAIN stock through colander into a bowl and then DISCARD the solid matter collected.
- DUMP the stock back into the pot. STRETCH cheesecloth over rinsed bowl and POUR stock through to collect finer particles.
- RINSE the pot.
- RETURN strained stock to pot and REDUCE by half.
- STORE stock in the refrigerator for a few days or freeze for up to a few months. Or move on to chowda or soup prep.

Fisherman's Tip

When you make stocks, less stirring is better. Let everything mellow in the pot. A quick stir when you add each new ingredient is plenty.

Yield: About 1½ quarts, depending on size of fish carcass.
Kitchen Time: Active 30 minutes. Simmer and reduction 2 hours.
In Season: Year-round.

Fish Tacos

Fish tacos can be served up any number of ways. Batter frying and heavy seasonings are perfectly delicious ways to create fish tacos, but sometimes in all the hoopla — you lose the fish! 'Our' way is simple, healthy and highlights the flavorful fish. Add on salsa, cheese, avocado and other 'fixins' of your choice — but the cabbage, white sauce and FRESH LOCAL FISH are a must!

The Catch
fresh fish fillets (estimate ½ pound per eater)

The Groceries
½ head of cabbage, shredded
⅓ cup mayonnaise
⅓ cup sour cream
1 teaspoon lime juice
½ teaspoon cumin
½ chicken bouillon cube, crumbled
1 teaspoon chipotle hot sauce
a little flour
garlic powder
black pepper
an egg
some milk
margarine (or canola oil)
corn tortillas (or flour tortillas, or hard taco shells)

The Extras
salsa, cheese and 'fixins' of your choosing.

The How To

- CUT fish into strips – think fish fingers. Scissors work great for this!
- WASH strips and DRY thoroughly with a paper towel.
- SALT them lightly on both sides and wait ten minutes. The salt 'sweats' the surface water out of the fish so that the flour will adhere evenly, and makes the crust firmer.

While you're waiting...

- BEAT an egg and two tablespoons-ish of milk together in a bowl for dredging the fish.
- MIX a little garlic powder, pepper, and flour in another bowl for dredging the fish.
- SHRED the cabbage into bite-size pieces big enough to be crunchy.
- MAKE the white sauce by mixing mayo, sour cream, lime juice, cumin, crumbled bouillon and hot stuff together.
- WARM your tortillas. (Microwaving 30 seconds with damp paper towel works for 'soft' taco shells. Heating in a low oven works for 'hard' taco shells.)
- FIND your fixins and get 'em ready! No one wants a cold taco...

Back to the fish...

- HEAT ¼ inch of oil in a skillet over medium heat – not high! (High heat will burn the fish before cooking it through.) Skillet is ready when a drop of water 'splatters' in oil.
- SPEAR each fish strip with a fork and DREDGE through the egg wash, then the seasoned flour, then the egg wash, then the seasoned flour. (The fork will keep your fingers from messing up the coating.)
- FORK fish into oil carefully. Ideally – you will move the fish only once, to flip it. The more you move it – the less crispy the crust.
- COOK it on the first side for 3-4 minutes, until it is dark golden brown, but not burned. FLIP with a fork.
- COOK on the second side until flaking the fish with a fork proves its meat opaque. (The second side will probably take 2-4 minutes depending on the thickness of the fish and your definition of 'medium heat.')
- FILL warmed tortillas/shells with fish, cabbage, liberal spoonfuls of white sauce and fixins! ENJOY immediately with a local cerveza!

Yield: Estimate ½ pound of fish per eater for dinner.
Kitchen Time: 30 minutes.
In Season: Year-round.

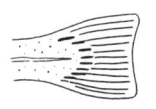

Flounder Francese

—Bob's way

Flaky fish, wilted spinach and restaurant-grade, rich lemon wine sauce — at home! This dish is 'fancy,' but really easy and fast!

"I'm strong to the finish cause I eats my spinach. — I'm Popeye the Sailor Man!"

The Catch
8-10 Flounder fillets
  (about 2 per eater)

The Groceries
¼ cup flour, seasoned with
  salt and pepper
2 eggs, beaten
2 Tablespoons canola oil
2 lemons, one thinly sliced,
  one squeezed for juice
zest of one lemon
1 cup white wine
1 Tablespoon cornstarch
2 Tablespoons water
2 Tablespoons capers, drained
1 pound baby spinach

Fisherman's Tip

Usually we estimate fish by the pound, but flounder fillets are a distinctive small size and we tend to just serve 2 per person.

The How To

- WASH your fish and PAT DRY with a paper towel.
- PREPARE two shallow bowls for dredging. The first should contain flour seasoned with salt, pepper and the zest from one of the lemons. The second should have two beaten eggs.
- BOIL two cups of water in a large pot with steamer basket inside.
- PREHEAT oven to 250°F.
- HEAT canola oil in a sauté pan over medium-high heat.
- DREDGE fillets in the flour, SHAKE off excess and DIP into the egg.
- PLACE immediately into your hot oiled pan and COOK until golden brown on one side, approximately 2-3 minutes. DO NOT DISTURB fish while cooking, so the coating gets crispy.
- TURN the fillet carefully and BROWN the other side in the same way, without disturbing the fish after turning.
- TRANSFER fillets from the pan to a large oven-proof platter. STORE in oven to keep warm while you sauté your remaining fillets.

When all fillets have been sautéed and are warming in the oven...

- DROP spinach into steaming pot with steamer basket and cover.
- ADD the juice of 1 lemon and white wine to the pan you have been sautéing the fish in, over medium heat. SCRAPE up the crusty bits off the bottom of the pan. COOK until it starts to bubble.
- MAKE a slurry with 1 tablespoon cornstarch and 2 tablespoons water. STIR slurry into sauce, as well as capers and lemon slices.
- CONTINUE to cook for about a minute or until sauce begins to thicken slightly.
- REMOVE from heat.
- CHECK on your spinach. If it appears to be cooking unevenly, TOSS it with tongs to expose the raw leaves to the steam.
- PLATE your meal. Using tongs, PLACE a serving of spinach in the center of each plate. TOP the spinach with two fillets perpendicular to each other and slightly overlapping. SPOON sauce over the fish and spinach. GARNISH with a cooked lemon slice. SERVE immediately.

Yield: Dinner for 4. Estimate 2-3 fillets per eater (less than ½ pound).

Kitchen Time: 25 minutes.

In Season: Year-round.

Grilled Whole Fish

We feel silly saying it, but this is a succulent, primal, satisfying and strangely romantic way to eat a fish. Some eat the crispy, 'rotisserie chicken style' skin. Some peel it off. But everyone appreciates the smoky flavor and lack of waste.

The Catch

fresh whole fish 2 inches thick or thicker, gutted and scaled, but otherwise intact (estimate 2 pounds per eater)

The Groceries

Per 2 pounds of fish:

½ of one lemon, wedged
2 garlic cloves, smashed
a 'rub' that you like AND/OR a spicy, salty, oily marinade if you're cooking tomorrow
canola oil

The Gear

small skewers or toothpicks

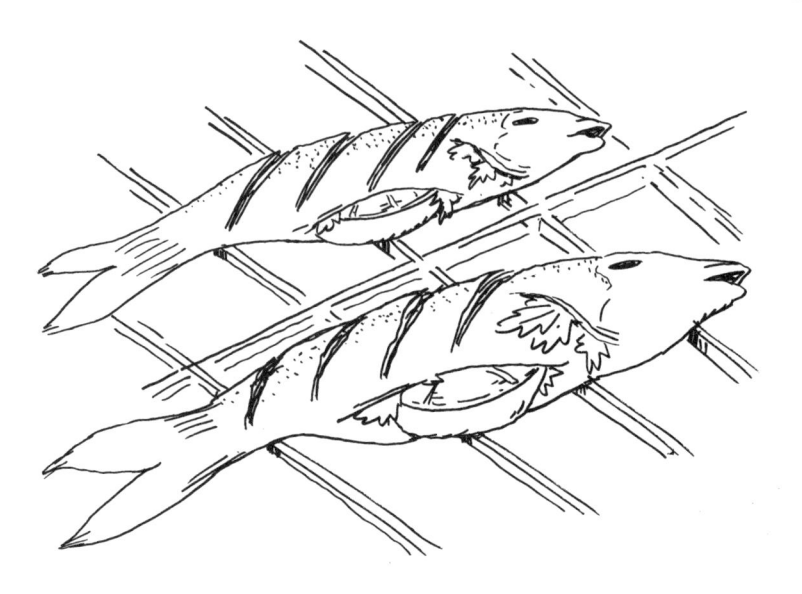

The How To

- RINSE your gutted, scaled fish and DRY thoroughly with paper towel.
- SLASH diagonal 'steam slits' parallel to the gill every two inches from gill to tail. The slits need to go all the way to the bone. This will help your fish cook evenly.
  (If you are marinating it overnight – PUT fish in a big ziplock bag with enough marinade to drown them and REFRIGERATE.)
- RUB the inside of all the steam slits with a 'rub' or season salt that you like.
- STUFF fish's cavity with smashed garlic cloves and then 'SEAL' the opening with lemon wedges, rind side out. USE toothpicks or skewers to keep the lemons in place.
- GREASE up your fish! SPREAD canola oil over all parts of the fish. Head, tail, skin, lemon, everything.
- HEAT up the grill to high.
- GREASE the side of the grill closest to you with an oiled paper towel pushed around by a spatula.
  (Your fish is going to be 'rolled' away from you not 'flipped' and so needs room to roll backwards.)
  Immediately PLACE the fish on the greased spot.
- REDUCE heat to 'medium.' CLOSE the grill's cover and WAIT.
- CALCULATE approximately 10 minutes of cooking per each inch of fish's thickness. So, if your fish is 2 inches thick it will take about 20 minutes, 10 per side. Therefore, don't even think of flipping until _at least_ 10 minutes. During that time – do not wiggle your fish, adjust your fish, or play with your fish. Movement makes the skin fall off.
- GREASE up the top side of the fish with another oily paper towel.
- NUDGE any stuck skin off the grill gently with a greasy spatula.
- ROLL your fish towards the back of the grill with two spatulas. CLOSE the grill cover.
- COOK the second side a few minutes less than the first side.
- WHEN time's up, gently NUDGE any stuck skin off the grill with a greasy spatula.
- LIFT your fish off the grill with two spatulas and PLACE on a serving platter with the cooked lemon wedges and garlic on top. DIG IN and don't be shy!

Fisherman's Tip:
If you are not sure how long to cook your fish, cut a 'peeking flap' in the side of the fish that will be grilled first. Then you can 'peek' at the meat without disturbing your fish.

To cut the 'flap,' slice along the spine from one steam slit to the next at the thickest part of the fish. Place the fish on the grill flap side down and facing you. When the meat viewed inside this 'flap' is opaque, that side of the fish is done and it's time to 'roll'.

Yield: Estimate 2 pounds whole fish per eater.
Kitchen Time: Prep 10 minutes. Grill 20+ minutes. Marinate overnight optional.
In Season: Year-round.

Portuguese Baked Blackfish

– Robby's way

This incredibly simple dish weaves veggies and fish together wonderfully. Tautog is thick enough to absorb flavors while keeping its own intact. Five minutes of preparation leads to a gourmet meal!

The Catch
2 pounds Blackfish (Tautog) fillets

The Groceries
1 28-ounce can stewed tomatoes
1 large green pepper, sliced long
1 onion, sliced into rings

The Gear
tinfoil

The Extras
seasoned rice

The How To

- PREHEAT oven to 350°F.
- SPREAD layer of tomatoes and most of pepper slices and onion rings in the bottom of a 9 x 9 inch baking dish.
- PLACE fish fillets on top.
- COVER with remaining tomatoes, pepper slices and onion rings.
- SEAL baking dish tightly with tinfoil.
- BAKE at 350°F for 45 minutes.
- SERVE with seasoned rice.

Yield: Dinner for 6.
Kitchen Time: Active 5 minutes. Bake 45 minutes.
In Season: April through December.

Portuguese Fish Chowder

-from Anthony's Seafood

Anthony's Seafood is an island institution. What started as a fish-house on the docks of Newport is now one of the island's few 'roll up your sleeves and dig in' casual seafood eateries. The local Portuguese influence spices up this hearty chowder!

*Shrimp are not local to Newport, but as Anthony's is a seafood market they can get tasty Gulf shrimp easily, which is how shrimp snuck into this beloved island recipe. (Sneaky shrimp...)

The Catch
1 pound Cod fillets
10 ounces Sea or Bay Scallops
4 cups clam juice

The Groceries
½ pound raw small shrimp (70/90 count)*
1 medium potato
1 Tablespoon butter
½ stalk celery, diced
¼ onion, chopped
½ pound hot link chouriço, casing removed, diced
½ cup white wine
¼ teaspoon red pepper flakes
heavy dash black pepper
1 Tablespoon tabasco
½ Tablespoon paprika
⅓ cup flour
4 sprigs fresh parsley, chopped fine
3 cups half & half

The Extras
oyster crackers

The How To

- QUARTER unpeeled potatoes and BOIL in two cups of clam juice until just fork tender. COOL and DICE.
- SLICE Sea Scallops and Cod into bite-sized pieces. No need to cut up shrimp or Bay Scallops.
- MELT butter in big pot on medium high.
- ADD celery, onions and chouriço. SAUTÉ until vegetables are translucent and have taken on some yellow color from the chouriço grease. ADD red pepper flakes, pepper, paprika, and tabasco.
- DEGLAZE pan with white wine, scraping off any browned bits.
- REDUCE heat to low. STIR in flour to make a roux of peanut butter consistency. COOK two minutes to activate the flour's gluten.
- ADD two cups clam juice and STIR vigorously. The roux will be inclined to stick to the sausage. You must get it into the liquid to help this chowder thicken.
- Once the base has thickened some, (a couple minutes) ADD shrimp, scallops and fish. BRING TO a simmer.
- ADD parsley and cooked potatoes.
- STIR in half & half. When 'simmer bubbles' reappear, SIMMER five minutes to thicken chowder, stirring and scraping the bottom regularly to avoid burning.
- SERVE with oyster crackers.

Yield: 10-12 'cup-sized' servings.
Kitchen Time: About an hour.
In Season: Year-round.

Sweet & Sour Monkfish Stir-Fry over Coconut Rice

Monkfish meat is somewhere between fish, lobster and scallops. Its firm texture holds up well in kabobs as well as stir-frys. Pick up some sweet and sour sauce the next time you have fresh monkfish and enjoy this tangy dish over sumptuous coconut rice!

The Catch
1 pound Monkfish fillets

The Groceries
1 13.5-ounce can coconut milk

1½ cup white rice

1 teaspoon salt

canola oil

2 Tablespoons flour

3 small onions

1 red pepper

¼ cup sweet & sour sauce

Fisherman's Tip

When Monkfishermen don't feel like cooking, they head to "The Fifth Element" on Broadway. The Fifth buys a lot of local monkfish and Chef Chris DePerro creates succulent 'bone-in' recipes. (One is up on fishermanstable.com)

The How To

- HEAT coconut milk, one coconut milk can-full of water (13.5 ounces), and a teaspoon of salt to boiling in a sauce pan with a lid.
- ADD rice and REDUCE heat to lowest setting. COVER and COOK for 25 minutes. USE this time to prep stir fry ingredients. When rice has ten minutes left to cook, START fish.
- PEEL onions leaving the 'root end' or, 'circle you usually trim off,' intact. SLICE onions in half from the stem end to the root end. Then SLICE each half into four wedges in this same direction. By leaving the root intact, the wedges will not fall apart during cooking.
- CUT pepper into big chunks.
- WASH Monkfish and DRY with a paper towel. CUT Monkfish into one inch thick nuggets. DUST nuggets lightly with flour. SHAKE OFF excess.
- HEAT one tablespoon canola oil over medium high heat in a large skillet with sides. Skillet is ready when a drop of water 'splatters' in oil. ADD monkfish nuggets and COOK without disturbing for 2½ minutes. Edges should form a golden brown crust.
- TURN nuggets with fork and COOK for 2½ more minutes. SET ASIDE.
- ADD one more tablespoon oil to skillet over medium high heat. ADD onions and peppers and COOK two minutes without disturbing. (This gives them the chance to brown.) TOSS and COOK two more minutes.
- ADD Monkfish and sweet & sour sauce and TOSS gently, scraping any stuck bits off the pan. COOK for one minute or until fish is heated through.
- SERVE heaped over coconut rice.

Yield: Dinner for 4.
Kitchen Time: 30 minutes.
In Season: Year-round.

Sweet Potato Fish Cakes with Lemon & Garlic Sour Cream

Extra fish, fish leftovers, fish scraps, and (yes!) day old Bluefish, are all transformed into succulent, delicious dinner with this 'quick and dirty' recipe. They freeze wonderfully!

The Catch
2 cups of fish you want to get rid of, cooked or uncooked

The Groceries
Fish Cakes:
2 Tablespoons butter*
¼ cup chopped onion*
(*if starting with raw fish)
1 sweet potato
2 sleeves of 'saltine' crackers
2 Tablespoons lemon juice (more if it is a SUPER fishy fish)
a handful of scallions, chopped
1 egg
1 Tablespoon of a 'season salt' you like (Montreal Steak, Mrs Dash, Mesquite...)
canola oil

Lemon & Garlic Sour Cream:
1 clove garlic, minced fine
Kosher salt
2 teaspoons lemon juice
½ cup sour cream

The Extras
simple green salad

The How To

*If you are starting with raw fish...
- SAUTÉ the fish in butter & onion until done.

If you're using leftover fish, start here...
- POKE the sweet potato with a fork, WRAP it in a wet paper towel and MICROWAVE it for 2 minutes at a time, until soft.
- SMUSH the crackers into medium-sized crumbs, not dust. (A no-mess way is to put into a gallon-sized ziplock bag and smash.)
- COOL the fish and sweet potato then CRUMBLE them into ½ inch chunks.
- COMBINE in a large bowl with lemon juice, scallions, seasoning, and egg. MIX with a fork until uniformly wet and lumpy.
- ADD in cracker crumbs and MIX with a fork or your hands.
- FORM sticky 'cakes' with your hands, ½ inch thick and 3-4 inches round. If cakes won't hold together - add another egg. If too gooey, add more crackers.
- PUT some flour on a plate and PAT each cake into flour before cooking. This will help it form a crust.
- HEAT a few tablespoons canola oil in a skillet over medium heat. When oil is hot enough that a drop of water splatters, ADD the fish cakes.
- COOK cakes 3 minutes a side, until golden brown. Don't move them around so a crust will form. Before removing from heat, TEST one by poking it through the middle to make sure it is hot through.
- SERVE with a dollop of 'Lemon and Garlic Sour Cream,' over a simple green salad.

To make Lemon & Garlic Sour Cream...
- SPRINKLE minced garlic with 2 pinches of Kosher salt in a small bowl. MIX it up and let it sit for a minute. The salt will start to pull the moisture from the garlic. With the back of a wooden spoon, GRIND the bits against the side of the bowl for a solid minute to turn the garlic into as fine a gel as you can get. The salt will help mash it up.
- STIR in sour cream.
- STIR in lemon juice, one teaspoon at a time – to taste.

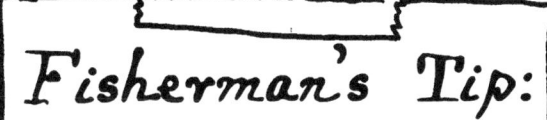

> **Fisherman's Tip:**
> If freezing fish cakes, don't dust with flour. Freeze on wax paper for 1 hour, then put into a ziplock bag, squeezing as much air out as possible. They will keep for about 3 months. Thaw in the fridge for a day or on the counter for 2 hours. Don't thaw in microwave. Dust with flour and cook normally.

Yield: Dinner for 8 or 10-12 cakes.
Kitchen Time: 25 minutes.
In Season: Year-round.

About Lobster...

Someone, somewhere, long ago, looked at the slick, complicated, many legged body of a lobster and thought the improbable: "*I bet I could eat that...*" Thank heavens. Lobster is now craved as a summer ritual, a vacation must-have, and a decadent treat. But local lobster is so much more than that! Lobsters are plentiful in the waters off Aquidneck Island in summer AND winter, creating a year-round fishery in need of eaters! Lobster meat is as healthy as chicken and can be succulent in so many ways, even without a side of melted butter...

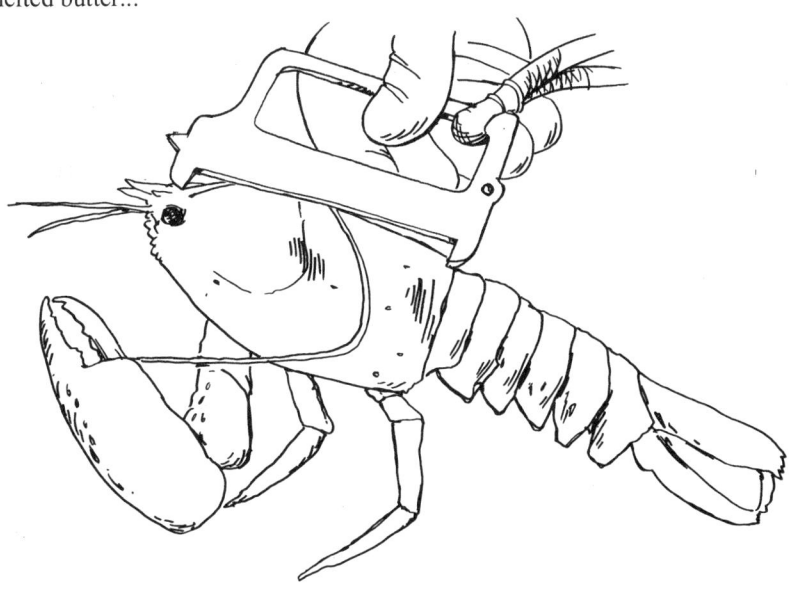

The Local Catch

'Clawed American lobster' *(Homarus americanus)* thrives in the cold water of the Atlantic, and is known for its delicate claw and tail meat. 'Spiny' clawless lobsters aren't a local species, or even a close relative of the Atlantic's clawed lobsters. The closest relative to our local lobster is something more like a crayfish, found in warmer waters.

Lobstering in Rhode Island requires a license, either recreational or commercial. Commercial vessels in RI waters must always be 'owner operated,' (with the license holder on board during any fishing) and each commercial license holder can only fish a maximum of 800 traps. These restrictions create an industry absolutely dependent on the individual small-boat fisherman; an industry that needs year-round, hungry support!

Which is which?

Local lobsters are all of one species, but there are different kinds. 'Chickens,' 'culls,' 'bullets,' 'selects,' and 'new shells' are all terms you will hear. The different names refer to size, number of claws, and hardness of shell – but not in that order... 'Roe' and 'tomalley,' will also come up in conversation. To some they are delicacies. To others...not so much. 'Sand sacs' and the 'dark line running down the middle of the lobster's tail' are the only parts that one really shouldn't eat.

'New Shells...' Every so often, lobsters 'molt' and create a new shell in order to grow. Just after that molting their 'new shells' are quite soft and their meat is very, very tender. These 'soft' lobsters do not contain as much meat as their harder peers, but they are easy to peel with just your fingers. Soft shell lobsters are truly a sea-side treat; as they do not survive long outside of the water, they do not get shipped to inland stores.

'Hard shell' lobsters have had lots of time (maybe years!) after molting to get their shells into thick fighting trim. Hammers, nut-crackers, cleavers and pliers are all tools that might be called on to 'crack' through to the meat inside. Hard shell lobster meat is more defined and firmer than 'softies.' As they can survive for a long time out of the ocean, they are widely distributed in non-coastal regions.

'Chicken' lobsters or 'Chix' are generally the smallest legal size (though, lobster 'size' is actually measured by the length of the carapace, rather than weight). They weigh under 1¼ pounds and are often sold at a different rate than bigger lobsters as they yield less 'meat per pound' than a lobster with the same amount of body, but bigger claws and tail.

'Culls' are lobsters with only one claw. New England lobsters are a contentious bunch (think Red Sox vs. Yankees). Fighting is part of the game and sometimes claws come off! Lobsters generally have two claws: the 'crusher' (big and blunt) and the 'cutter' or 'shredder' (small and sharp). Each claw does what its name says. Lobsters are able to regenerate their claws during their next molting. Culls can be missing either claw.

'*Bullets*' or '*Tails*' are lobsters who have lost both claws. They flock to lobster traps for meals they can get without their hands.

'*Selects*' are 'Grade A,' nice looking lobsters – generally one and a half pounds or more. Big claws, hard shell, lots of meat.

'*Roe*' are lobster eggs sometimes found at the top of a lobster's tail meat. Uncooked roe is black. Cooked it turns bright, bright orange. It is considered a delicacy.

'*Tomalley*' is the greenish stuff inside the lobster's body. It might not be the healthiest thing for you, but is packed with lobster flavor. Using a little of it in stocks or sauces packs a salty lobster punch.

'*Sand Sacs*' are actually the lobster's stomach, located right behind the eye sockets. They are easily pulled out and should be discarded.

'*The dark line running down the middle of the lobster's tail*' is exactly what you think it is. We throw that out too.

Lobster 'Math'

2 'chicken' lobsters yield about 1 cup meat.

Kitchen Musts:

Steam, never boil.
Don't overcook.

Basic Steamed Lobster	74
Char-grilled Lobster 'Bullets'	76
Lobster & Crab Bisque	78
Lobster 'Fra Diavlo'	80
Lobsterman's Mac 'n' Cheese	82
Lobsterman's Pie	84
Lobster or Crab Stock	86
Lobster Scampi over Fresh Spinach Pasta	88
Lobster Stuffed Lobster	90
Soft Lobster Boats	92

Basic Steamed Lobster

— Eric's way

The most common question we get on the docks is, "How do YOU cook lobster?" Answer — like this.

The Catch
live local lobster
> (estimate 2 pounds per eater for dinner)

The Groceries
1 'shot' vinegar, optional

The Gear
big pot with a steamer basket

Fisherman's Tip:

You are basing your 'time' on the average weight of the lobsters. If they are generally the same, great. If you are cooking a 3 lb lobster in the same pot as a 1 lb lobster, you will need to take one out early. These directions are good for cooking between 1-5 lobsters.

<u>Please</u> don't overcook your lobster. It makes them rubbery and gives us a bad name.

The How To

- BOIL one inch of water in a big pot that has a tight lid and a steamer basket. Optional: ADD a shot of white vinegar to make the shells brittle and the shucking easier.
- DROP in the lobsters and COVER tightly.
- BRING water back to a boil, then START TIMING. (Often with a steamer basket, the water never stops boiling.) If you are planning on 're-cooking' lobster in a dish – subtract a couple of minutes from their steaming time.

    STEAMING TIMING:

    To determine your lobster's 'hardness,' hold the body and squeeze. If it is collapsible to where you feel you could do damage just by squeezing – it is a 'soft shell.' If it has only a little 'springy' give – then it is a 'medium shell.' If it has no give whatsoever and feels like a rock – it is a 'hard shell.'

    - 1 pound lobsters: soft shell = 8 minutes; hard shell = 10 minutes
    - 1 ½ pound lobsters: soft shell = 13 minutes; hard shell = 15 minutes
    - 2 pound lobsters: soft shells = 17 minutes; hard shell = 19 minutes

- MELT butter and PREPARE the table and 'sides' while lobsters are steaming. Each guest should have his or her own small dish of 'rinse' water and melted butter.
- REMOVE lobsters when time is up with tongs and/or a rubber glove. They should be bright red all over and claws should pull off easily.
- HOLD the lobster red side down on a firm surface and SLIT the tail up the middle with a big knife. This will make it easier for your guests. WHACK each claw crosswise with a big knife, deep enough to crack it, to make it easy for your guests.
- SERVE the steaming lobsters immediately! No waiting, no passing go, no collecting 200 anythings.

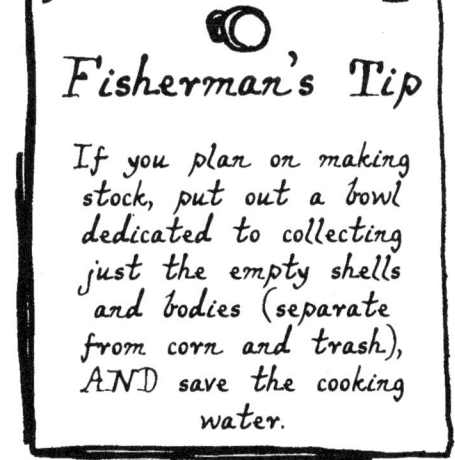

> **Fisherman's Tip**
>
> If you plan on making stock, put out a bowl dedicated to collecting just the empty shells and bodies (separate from corn and trash), AND save the cooking water.

Yield: Estimate 2 pounds of whole lobster per eater for dinner.

Kitchen Time: 20 minutes.

In Season: Year-round.

Char-grilled Lobster Bullets

Though steaming is our favorite method for cooking whole lobster, on those rare summer days when fishermen get home in time to fire up the grill, char-grilled lobster meat is an incredible treat. We tend to grill the 'bullet' (clawless) lobsters as the tail is really what benefits from the smoke.

The Catch
live lobster 'Bullets' (or tails)

The Groceries
(For up to 6 lobsters)

½ cup olive oil

1 teaspoon dill

1 lemon, squeezed

2 cloves garlic, minced

black pepper to taste

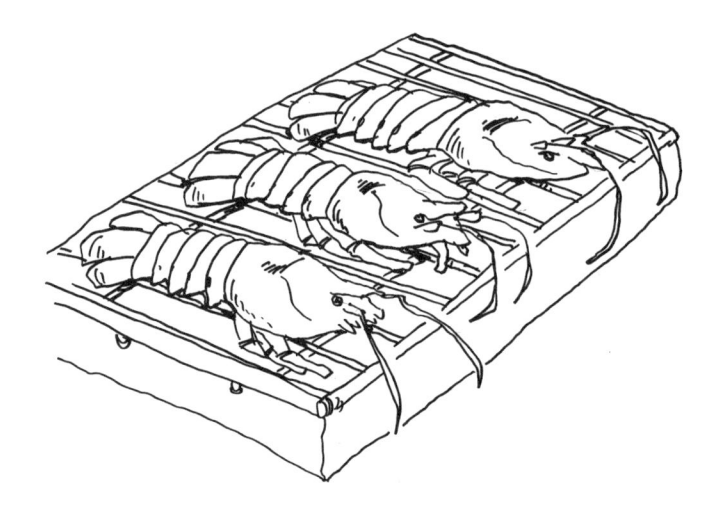

The Gear
skewers

> **Fisherman's Tip**
>
> As flame is key – charcoal grills are the best, gas is okay, and electric doesn't work.

The How To

- FIRE up your grill to medium.
- MIX the oil, dill, lemon, garlic and pepper together.
- GET your biggest knife and your fish cutting board.
- BUTTERFLY your uncooked lobsters: Shell side down, insert a big knife at the head, and slice all the way to the end of the tail meat, without going through the back of the shell.
- LEAVE in the tomalley (green stuff you will see in body).
- REMOVE and DISCARD sand sacs from behind the eyes and the tube running down the center of tail.
- SKEWER each tail lengthwise so it won't 'curl up' during cooking.
- IF your lobsters do have claws, CRACK the claws with your knife so steam will be able to get out.
- BASTE the tail meat heavily with the oil mixture.
- GRILL over medium-high heat, meat side up, 6-8 minutes for 'average' sized lobsters. (Bullets are hard to describe by weight.) BASTE continuously and let some oil drip so the grill will 'flame up' and give that smoky flavor. Shell should be bright red before you flip.
- FLIP with tongs.
- BASTE the shells, and cook for 6-8 more minutes. Lobsters are done when tail meat is creamy white and opaque and when antennae pull off easily.
- SERVE with a lemon wedge.

Yield: Estimate 2-3 bullets per eater for dinner or 1 per eater as appetizer.
Kitchen Time: Prep 10 minutes. Grill 15 minutes.
In Season: Year-round.

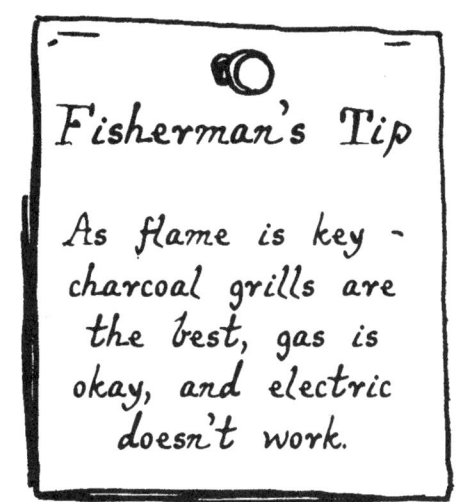

Lobster & Crab Bisque

This is a pretty sumptuous way to 'get the most' out of your shellfish. Unlike many of its peers, this bisque gets its richness from the lobster and crab, rather than heavy cream. Serve guilt free!

The Catch

1 lobster, steamed (page 74)

6 crabs, steamed (page 38)

8 cups of LOBSTER OR CRAB STOCK (page 86)

The Groceries

2 Tablespoons butter

2 medium onions, chopped

2 carrots, chopped

2 celery stalks, chopped

2 Tablespoons tomato paste

½ cup white wine

4 Tablespoons flour

1 bay leaf

2 sprigs of thyme

2 stalks fresh parsley

10 peppercorns

2 garlic cloves, crushed

2 Tablespoons Madeira

½ cup half & half

2 dashes paprika

cayenne pepper to taste

The Gear

'china cap' or coarse strainer

cheesecloth

food processor

blender

The How To

- MELT butter over medium heat in your biggest pot.
- COOK onions, carrots, and celery until softened.
- HARVEST the meat from the lobster tail and claws, and crab claws. SET ASIDE.
- PULL OFF the little legs of the lobsters, and the little claws of the crabs. ADD to pot.
- CARAMELIZE all over medium high heat until slightly brown but not burnt.
- ADD tomato paste and continue cooking for 30 seconds.
- DEGLAZE the bottom of the pan with white wine and SCRAPE off all the stuck bits.
- SPRINKLE in 4 tablespoons of flour. STIR to make a 'roux' of peanut butter consistency.
- ADD in a few cups of LOBSTER OR CRAB STOCK (86) and whisk to make sure anything stuck on the bottom of the pan comes up.
- PUT bay leaf, thyme, parsley and peppercorns in a cheesecloth 'sachet.' ADD to pot. BRING to simmer.
- SIMMER one hour. SKIM off foam and any formed 'skin' if so inclined.
- DISCARD spice 'sachet.' STRAIN all through a 'china cap' or coarse strainer.
- GRIND the solids as much as possible in a food processor.
- RETURN whole mixture to simmer for ten minutes.
- STRAIN all again, SQUISHING moisture through strainer lined with cheesecloth.
- BLEND 1 cup broth and meat in blender on high until smooth. RETURN to pot.
- ADD 2 Tablespoons Madeira, and salt and black pepper to taste.
- SIMMER 5 minutes.
- ADD ½ cup half & half and cayenne pepper to taste.
- TOP with paprika for color, if desired. SERVE.

Yield: 9 cups or 4 bowls.
Kitchen Time: Active 30 minutes. Simmer 1 hour.
In Season: Year-round.

Lobster 'Fra Diablo'

― by Bill Solitro

Literally translated to: "Fire of the Devil", this flashy dish is actually not that hard to make.
Tons of lobster and shellfish in a spicy marinara sauce! Cooking the shellfish in the marinara allows flavors to mingle, resulting in a sauce that is richly unique.
Impress your dinner guests with this 'fiery' restaurant favorite!

The Catch
8 uncooked lobsters
3 pounds mussels
20-24 Littlenecks

The Groceries
96 ounces marinara sauce
    (4 24-ounce jars)
3 Tablespoons sugar
misc. spices for marinara
1 head garlic, peeled and chopped
olive oil
red pepper flakes
dried oregano
dried basil
1 cup Italian red wine

The Extras
2 pounds linguine
fresh crusty bread

The How To

- BREAK tails and claws off uncooked lobsters. SAVE the bodies and all their juice. REMOVE sand sacs behind the eyes.
- CUT tails into two the long way, severing completely. DISCARD dark tube.
- SIMMER marinara sauce on low in the biggest pot you have. ADD in 3 tablespoons sugar and miscellaneous spices to taste.
- HEAT a few tablespoons olive oil on medium in the biggest sauté pan possible (like a huge iron skillet).
- ADD in red pepper flakes, garlic, sprinkles of oregano & basil, and lobster tails - meat side down.
- COOK undisturbed for two minutes. FLIP. COOK undisturbed for 2 more minutes. SCRAPE all (lobsters, garlic, oil, etc) into marinara.
- START AGAIN with heated olive oil, garlic, oregano, basil and red pepper. ADD claws and bodies. COOK for 2 minutes a side. SCRAPE all into marinara.
- TASTE the marinara every so often to check on its spice and ADJUST the amounts of garlic, oregano, basil and red pepper used in your sauté method accordingly.
- START AGAIN with heated olive oil, garlic, oregano, basil and red pepper. ADD in mussels. COOK, STIRRING every so often until they are slightly open, not all the way. SCRAPE all into marinara. REPEAT with Littlenecks.
- SIMMER sum total for about 30 minutes. TASTE after ten minutes, ADJUST seasonings and ADD wine.
- COOK linguine so it is ready at the same time.
- SERVE in a communal dish with huge ladles and a bowl of passed linguine.

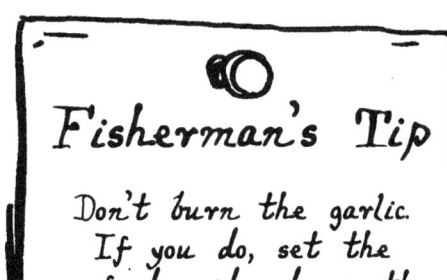

> **Fisherman's Tip**
>
> Don't burn the garlic. If you do, set the seafood aside, dump the pan and start again with fresh olive oil. Burned garlic messes up the whole show.

Yield: Dinner for 8-12.
Kitchen Time: 1 hour.
In Season: Year-round.

Lobsterman's Mac 'n' Cheese

There are three rules of Lobsterman's Mac 'n' cheese:

1. Don't overcook your lobster, steam them a few minutes less than done.
2. There should be at least a 1-1 ratio of lobster meat to pasta.
3. Use mild cheese so the lobster comes through!

The Catch

3 'chicken' lobsters OR 2 bigger lobsters, steamed till almost done (page 74) (1½-2 cups meat)

The Groceries

1½ cups uncooked 'medium-sized' pasta (macaroni, bow ties, etc.)
½ stick butter
¼ cup all-purpose flour
1 cup milk
½ teaspoon ground mustard
½ teaspoon black pepper
1 cup shredded mozzarella cheese
1 cup 'stronger' but still mild cheese (Monterey Jack, Mild Cheddar...)
½ cup sour cream
2 Tablespoons butter
½ cup seasoned breadcrumbs

The How To

- HARVEST lobster meat and cut into bite-sized chunks. SET ASIDE.
- BOIL water for pasta.
- PUT macaroni in, COVER and SHUT OFF heat. TIME for 10 minutes then DRAIN.
- TURN broiler on 'low' if you have a 'low.' If not – high works.

Meanwhile...

- MELT ½ stick butter in a large saucepan over medium heat.
- STIR in flour until it is a smooth, peanut butter consistency and it bubbles a little.
- WHISK in milk gradually. ADD mustard and pepper.
- SIMMER stirring constantly for 2 minutes or until thickened and whisk lines stay visible.
- TURN heat to low.
- STIR in cheese and HEAT until it looks just melted.
- REMOVE from heat.
- STIR in sour cream, drained macaroni and lobster chunks.
- TRANSFER to greased 9 x 9 baking dish.
- MELT 2 tablespoons butter. MIX with seasoned breadcrumbs. SPRINKLE on top of mac 'n' cheese.
- BROIL until breadcrumbs are golden brown. (Watch it closely – it can be as little as 3 minutes!)
- SHUT OFF broiler and move casserole to lower rack. Let it continue to warm for 10 minutes. SERVE and accept praise!

Yield: Dinner for 4.
Kitchen Time: Active 10 minutes. Oven 15 minutes.
In Season: Year-round.

Lobsterman's Pie

We have no words for how good this recipe is. Rich and buttery, packed with lobster and a thick creamy sauce. Similar to the taste of Lobster Newberg...but a little easier.

Pray for a raw, foggy day and an excuse to make it!

Fisherman's Tip

Though we highly recommend making lobster stock as it is flavorful like nothing else - you can 'cheat' by mixing 1 tablespoon of tomalley into 2 cups chicken stock.

The Catch
2-3 'chicken' lobsters, undercooked (1 cup meat)
½ pound of any white fish, raw, cut into 1 inch chunks

The Groceries
pie crust for 9 inch, 2 crust pie
½ stick butter
1 onion, chopped roughly
3 cloves garlic, minced
½ cup flour
2 cups LOBSTER OR CRAB STOCK
1 teaspoon dried tarragon
1 8-ounce package 'baby bella' mushrooms, halved
2 Tablespoons Madeira or sherry
double splash half & half
black pepper to taste

The Extras:
4 sweet potatoes, mashed

The How To

- PREHEAT oven to 400°F.
- HARVEST lobster meat and CUT into bite-sized chunks.
- PREPARE your pie crust.
- LINE a 9 inch pie plate, or square 9 x 9 pan with bottom crust.
- MELT ½ stick butter over medium heat in big saucepan.
- SOFTEN onions for a minute or two.
- ADD garlic and COOK for 30 seconds to wake up flavor.
- ADD in ½ cup flour and mix well to make a 'roux' of a peanut butter consistency. ADD more butter if not all the flour gets wet. COOK briefly until it 'bubbles.'
- WHISK the LOBSTER OR CRAB STOCK (page 86) into the 'roux.' ADD tarragon and mushrooms. THICKEN by stirring over low heat until the lines of the whisk stay visible in the sauce.
- ADD Madeira and double splash half & half and STIR.
- ADD lobster and fish chunks and MIX.
- DUMP the whole thing into the waiting pie crust.
- SPREAD other crust on top and PINCH edges to seal.
- CUT generous slits in crust big enough for steam to escape!
- COOK at 400°F until bubbly and crust is brown, at least 25 minutes but probably 30-35. (Can put tinfoil around edges if they get dark before bubbling.)
- COOL for 20 minutes before serving so juices thicken.
- SERVE with mashed sweet potatoes.

Yield: Dinner for 6.

Kitchen Time: Active 15 minutes, plus prepping pie crust. Bake 30-35 minutes.

In Season: Year-round.

Lobster or Crab Stock

Delicious soups and sauces can be made out of the shells you were about to throw out. Try making stock to get every bit of goodness out of your crustacean treat. Lobster and crab are mild flavors and this recipe is careful to not overpower them with vegetables so their flavor comes through!

The Catch
bodies, shells & little legs of:
- 3-4 lobsters
- OR 10 or so crabs
- OR a combo

water used to steam lobsters and crabs

The Groceries
1 stalk celery, chopped (½ cup)
1 carrot, chopped (½ cup)
1 onion, chopped (1 cup)
4 Tablespoons olive oil
1 clove garlic, chopped
1 handful of fresh parsley, chopped (¼ cup)
¼ cup Madeira
2 sprigs fresh thyme (½ teaspoon dried)
10 peppercorns
1 bay leaf
1½ teaspoons dried tarragon

The Gear
cheesecloth

The How To

- CRUSH and SMUSH up the bodies and shells of the lobsters and crabs as much as you can so they will fit in the pot. DISCARD sand sacs behind eyes, but KEEP all the greenish goo in the bodies as it adds a ton of flavor. SET ASIDE.
- HEAT oil on medium in your biggest pot.
- ADD in celery, carrots and onion and COOK for about 5 minutes.
- ADD lobster or crab bodies and COOK for 5 minutes.
- ADD garlic and parsley and COOK for 5 minutes.
- ADD wine and SCRAPE off any good brown stuff that might have stuck to the sides and/or bottom of the pot.
- POUR in the water you steamed the lobsters or crabs in and enough other water to cover solids by one inch.
- HEAT to a very low simmer – small bubbles should come up from the bottom every so often and steam should be constant.
- ADD spices.
- LOW SIMMER uncovered for 90 minutes. No need to stir too much. SKIM off foam if so inclined.
- GET OUT your biggest bowl, a colander and a mesh strainer or cheesecloth.
- POUR liquid and solid matter over colander into a bowl. DUMP the solid matter.
- STRAIN the broth through a fine mesh strainer or cheesecloth.
- STORE in the fridge in jars for up to 2 days, or FREEZE for up to a few months.

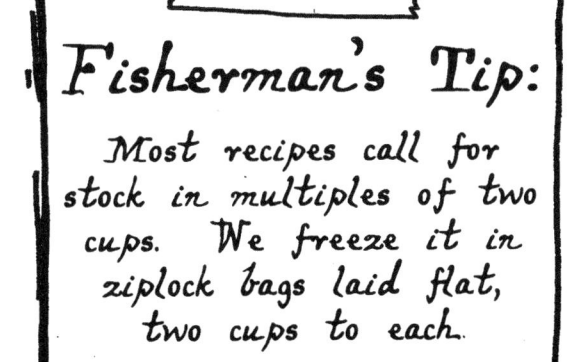

> **Fisherman's Tip:**
> Most recipes call for stock in multiples of two cups. We freeze it in ziplock bags laid flat, two cups to each.

Yield: 8-10 cups stock.
Kitchen Time: Active 30 minutes. Simmer 90 minutes.
In Season: Year-round.

Lobster Scampi over Fresh Spinach Pasta

This recipe manages to be light and sumptuous at the same time. We use fresh spinach pasta to sneak some vegetables in and because it goes so well with the sweet lobster meat! Recipe can be doubled and tripled — just remember, we like to estimate the meat of one 'chicken' size lobster per person. More never hurts...

The Catch

2 'chicken' lobsters, steamed till just done (page 74)

The Groceries

4 Tablespoons cold butter, divided in half
4 garlic cloves, chopped fine
2 Tablespoons lemon juice
1 Tablespoon Madeira
4 stalks fresh parsley, chopped
black pepper
fresh spinach linguine (9-ounce package is perfect)
¼ cup lobster or chicken stock

The How To

- HARVEST the lobster meat, chopping it into big chunks.
- READY other ingredients. This dish cooks very fast!
- BOIL salted pasta water in one pot. When pasta goes in, BEGIN sauce.
- SELECT a frying pan with tall enough edges to allow you to toss the pasta.
- MELT 2 tablespoons of butter over medium heat. When it stops foaming, ADD in garlic and COOK for 30 seconds.
- ADD in lobster chunks and ¼ cup lobster or chicken stock. WARM on medium for 1 minute.
- REMOVE from heat.
- STIR in lemon juice, 2 tablespoons cold butter, Madeira and parsley.
- TOSS with warm cooked spinach pasta.
- SEASON with black pepper to taste and SERVE.

Yield: Dinner for 2.
Kitchen Time: 25 minutes.
In Season: Year-round.

Lobster Stuffed Lobster

Not our healthiest dinner... but one that guests crave. The stuffing should be more seafood than breadcrumb to be sumptuously succulent.

Fisherman's Tip

If you're not keen on dispatching the live lobsters yourself, ask your fishmonger to do it for you. He should butterfly the lobsters, discard the sand sacs, and bag the tomalley for you.

The Catch

- 6 1½ pound live lobsters (4 to be stuffed, 2 for the stuffing)
- OR 4 1½ pound lobsters AND two cups 'other' seafood (crab, scallop, clam, fish), uncooked
- tomalley from one of the lobsters

The Groceries

- 1 cup onion, chopped
- 1 cup celery, chopped
- 2 cloves garlic, minced
- 2 teaspoons Worcestershire sauce
- 1 sleeve Ritz-style crackers, crumbled roughly
- 1 stick butter, melted

The Extras

- salad to start, to combat the butter...
- melted butter for serving

The How To

- MIX together in large bowl: crumbled crackers, chopped vegetables, minced garlic, melted butter and Worcestershire sauce. SET ASIDE.
- FIND a cookie sheet with sides or a large baking pan. LINE it with tinfoil. This is only to protect your pan from cooked-on mess. If using an old pan – skip it.
- PREHEAT oven to 375°F.
- GET OUT your fish cutting board and your big knife.
- BUTTERFLY four of your uncooked lobsters: Shell side down, insert a big knife at the head, and slice all the way to the end of the tail meat, without going through the back of the shell.
- REMOVE the tomalley (green stuff you will see in body) and SAVE it from one of the lobsters.
- REMOVE and DISCARD sand sacs from behind the eyes and tube running down center of tails.
- RINSE body cavities and SET ASIDE.
- HARVEST the meat from 2 other lobsters, OR other seafood (crabs, scallops, etc). Ideally you will have around 2 cups. CHOP into chunks no bigger than 1 inch.
- MIX this meat and the tomalley from one lobster into the stuffing, distributing the tomalley evenly as it is very salty.
- STUFF your lobsters: Fill the body cavities first, pressing firmly. If there is extra stuffing, spread the tail flat and stuff as much into the slit as you can.
- ARRANGE on pan, stuffing side up, head to tail, tail to head, to maximize room.
- COVER the whole pan with tinfoil, sealing it pretty well. This will keep the lobsters moist.
- BAKE at 375°F for 20 minutes. REMOVE the tinfoil.
- BAKE for another 5 minutes or until stuffing is slightly brown.
- SERVE hot, with a side of melted butter for ultimate decadence.

Yield: Dinner for 4.

Kitchen Time: Active 30 minutes. Bake 25 minutes.

In Season: Year-round.

Soft Lobster Boats

– Denny's way

Twice a year, lobsters 're-decorate' with new, soft shells. These shells are easy to peel with your fingers, eliminating the need for crackers and hammers.
By grilling these softies in tinfoil boats along with their rice and fixins — you will get a succulent, full meal with no mess!
Perfect for seaside camping!

The Catch
1 'soft' 'chicken' lobster per eater, plus a few extra!
6-8 Littlenecks per eater, scrubbed

The Groceries
Per Lobster:
¼ cup rice that doesn't take forever to cook
2 cloves garlic AND/OR ¼ onion, chopped
herbs of your choice
½ cup white wine
cooking spray or oil

The Gear
'heavy duty' tinfoil (or regular tinfoil, double layered)

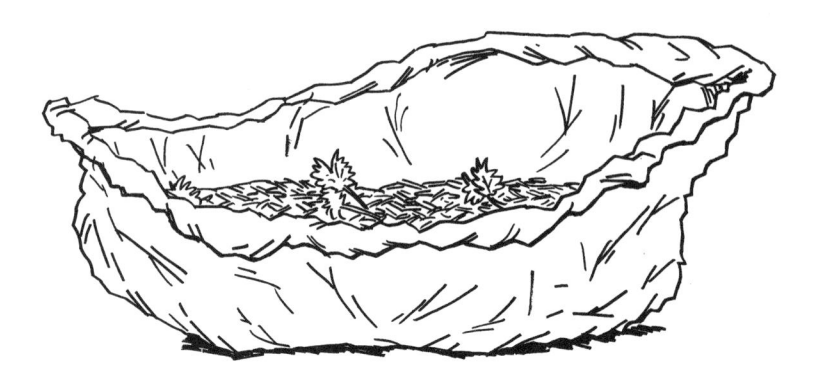

The How To

- HEAT up your grill to 'medium.'
- CHOP or mince up garlic, onions and herbs. SCRUB Littlenecks.
- RIP off a piece of 'heavy duty' tinfoil, 1½ times as long as it is deep and put it on the counter, long side closest to you. This tinfoil will be your lobster's 'boat.'
- SHAPE it into a 'boat' by pinching the bow's tinfoil together and curving it up. Same with the stern. (Think gondola.) The boat will need to hold water – so make sure all 'seams' are near the top.
- PAINT the inside bottom of the boat with cooking spray.
- LINE it with ¼ cup uncooked rice.
- ADD in garlic, onion, herbs...whatever you like.

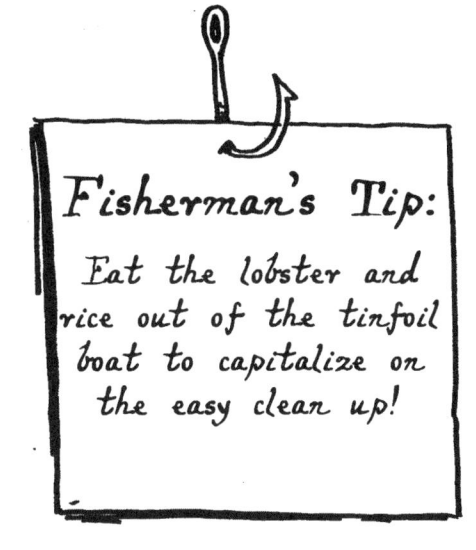

As soon as the grill is ready...

- PLACE your soft lobster into your boat and ARRANGE Littlenecks around lobster.
- CHRISTEN them with enough wine to make about ½ inch in the bottom of boat.
- SEAL up the top of the boat as best you can. POKE a hole in top so steam can escape.
- SAIL your boat on the medium-heat grill for about 15-20 minutes for a 'chicken' soft lobster. (Inspect the lobster to see that it is bright red all over and that antennae pull out easily. If you're nervous – give it two more minutes.)
- OPEN your boats carefully and ENJOY!

> **Fisherman's Tip:**
> Eat the lobster and rice out of the tinfoil boat to capitalize on the easy clean up!

Yield: Each boat is a light meal.
Kitchen Time: Prep 5 minutes. Grill 15 minutes.
In Season: Year-round.

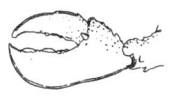

About Mussels, Oysters, Scallops and Squid...

Mussels, oysters, scallops and squid all grow around the island, but for various reasons the local varieties aren't widely available at the local markets. A great resource on where to find the local varieties is www.SeafoodRI.com. We've included a few recipes to highlight these ocean treasures.

Local Mussels...

With deep blue shells, bright orange meat, and a complete lack of sand, mussels are an attractive addition to any seafood lover's table. These bivalves are prized more for their tender texture than for their taste, which is very mild. This makes them perfect in assertive sauces and broths where they can absorb flavors. Don't forget the crusty bread to soak up the juice!

Blue mussels (Mytilus edulis) grow on pretty much any craggy seashore boulder, and Aquidneck Island has a few of those... However, most of the mussels you will find in the island's markets are farm-raised and not caught locally. Local mussels harvested in clean water are fine to eat, but beware! They often contain a small 'pearl,' so don't chomp down too hard.

Local Oysters...

Oysters are pretty much the taste of the ocean, in a shell. Briny, sexy, rich, salty. They are most often slurped raw, but can be grilled, fried and shucked into stew. Their meat is soft and silky. No one feels ambivalent about oysters. You either hate them or crave them as a decadent treat.

Our edible *True Oysters* are from the family *Osteidae*, different from their 'Pearl Oyster' cousins. They are fickle mollusks, with their environment needing to be 'just so' for them to survive. Fishermen have made strides towards understanding what makes them happy and local 'oysteries,' or oyster farms, are growing in popularity. As supply is still limited, most Rhody oysters are consumed in high-end restaurants or sold at farmers markets, rarely exported or found in chain stores.

Local Scallops...

Scallops are so cool. Beautiful underwater. Unbelievably tender on a plate. They have one hundred reflective eyes and the ability to swim (yes swim!) by opening and closing their shells. This swimming makes their adductor muscle (the part that holds the shell together) much larger than in other bivalves. That is the mild, pillowy part we eat.

Both **'Bay Scallops'** *(Argopecten irradians)* and **'Sea Scallops'** *(Placopecten magellanicus)* are found in RI waters. The most obvious difference is that Bay Scallops (caught near land) are little and Sea Scallops (caught off-shore) are big. When buying either type of scallop, you want them to be 'dry,' or untreated. Some fisheries treat scallops with sodium tripolyphosphate (STPP), a chemical that causes them to last longer as well as swell in size, fetching a higher price. These 'wet packed' scallops shrink during cooking and can have a medicinal flavor. If scallops don't have long to travel, there is no need for this preservative – so buy local, eat better!

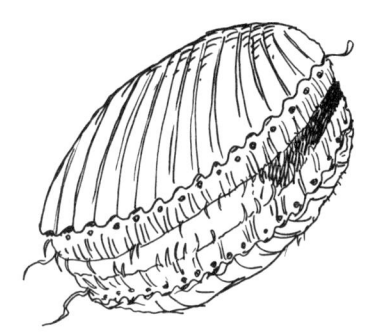

Local Squid...

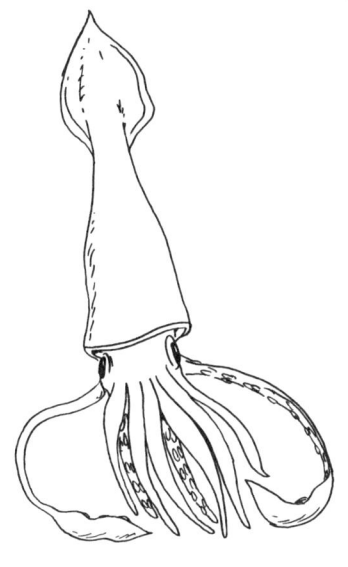

More squid are landed in Rhode Island than in any other state in the Northeast. Ironically, due to the popularity of this easily frozen seafood, there aren't always a lot held back to sell fresh in local markets. Fresh or frozen, squid, aka 'calamari,' has a unique 'bouncy' texture all its own. It's good fried, grilled, sautéed, stuffed, baked...

Local **'Long-Finned Squid'** *(loligo pealei)* are anywhere from 3 inches to a few feet long. They consist of tubes and tentacles – both of which are edible. The calamari 'rings' you see in restaurants are the squid's tubes, snipped into bite-size segments.

Twice a year squid come close to the island to 'spawn.' During this time the docks are packed elbow to elbow with recreational 'squid jiggers'...and their portable generators. As squid are attracted to light, fishermen point giant searchlights at the water to improve their chances of catching dinner. When squid are 'running,' barbeques and camper vans form a night-time village along the causeway to Goat Island as recreational squidders jig hopefully. The squid is a remarkable animal, and the amateur efforts taken to catch them are remarkable as well.

'Chinese 5-Spice' Calamari	98
Grilled Oysters Especial	100
Newport Scallops	102
Red Curried Mussels	104
Ricotta Stuffed Baby Squid	106
Tequila Lime Grilled Calamari	108

'Chinese 5-Spice' Calamari sautéed in brown butter

This recipe appeared in the Providence Journal, July 12, 2006 in a segment by Gail Ciampa titled "West Deck Calamari." Copyright © 2012 The Providence Journal. Reproduced by permission and with Chef Rob's consent.

— By Chef Rob Biela

Chef Rob is a die-hard Newporter and shares his talent at harbor restaurants. This recipe is a knockout and always on the menu at 'The Speakeasy' on Thames. Tender, tasty, unique calamari — not fried!

The Catch
1½ pounds squid tubes, cut into ½ inch rings

The Groceries
2 Tablespoons 'Chinese 5-spice' powder
½ cup almond slivers
½ cup dried currants
½ cup unsalted butter
2 cups cooked chickpeas
1 Tablespoon 'Sambal Chili' sauce
3 Tablespoons tahini paste
2 Tablespoons olive oil
2 Tablespoons water
salt, to taste
white pepper, to taste

The Extras
toasted or grilled pita bread triangles

The How To

- TOSS calamari in 'Chinese 5-spice' powder and marinate for five to ten minutes. SET ASIDE.
- TOAST almonds in the oven until golden brown. COOL almonds. COMBINE with black currants and SET ASIDE.
- COMBINE chick peas, chili sauce, tahini paste, olive oil, water, salt and pepper in food processor. PROCESS until smooth. SET ASIDE.
- HEAT butter over high in a large sauté pan until it turns brown.
- ADD the marinated calamari, currants and almonds. SAUTÉ 30-50 seconds only, until calamari is firm but not overcooked.
- CENTER the spicy hummus mixture in the middle of a large serving plate. POUR the calamari on top.
- GARNISH with toasted or grilled pita bread and serve.

Yield: Appetizer for 4.
Kitchen Time: 15 minutes.
In Season: Year-round.

Grilled Oysters 'Especial'
– Chris's way

Oysters are delicious-ioso raw, served only in the liquor they were born with. However, for good reason, raw seafood scares some folks. Laura's brother-in-law grills a mean oyster. Here's how...

The Catch
local oysters

The Groceries
olive oil
white wine
herbs (thyme, dill, etc.)
fresh parmesan cheese, grated

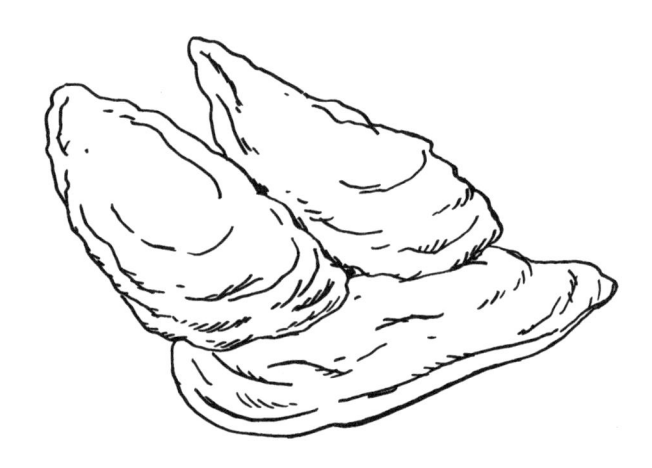

The How To

- SHUCK oysters with a dull knife: Leave the oyster in the shell, but dislodge it by sliding the knife under the meat. Leave the liquor.
- HEAT your grill to medium-high.
- MAKE a mixture of olive oil, white wine and whatever herbs you like, along with salt and pepper.
- DASH mixture on the oysters.
- GRILL oysters over medium-high heat, face up. DASH with the wine mixture every so often. For best results, allow some of the oil to get on the side of the shells to help the grill 'flame up.'
- REMOVE from heat when oysters are golden brown and look 'cooked.' Time depends entirely on grill temperature.
- SPRINKLE with grated parmesan cheese and SERVE.

Fisherman's Tip

RI has several great oysteries, farming mollusks packed with the rich, briny flavor of Narragansett Bay. If you are harvesting your own, as with any shellfish, be mindful of red-tide closings as advised on www.dem.ri.gov.

Yield: Appetizer.
Kitchen Time: Prep 5 minutes. Grill 10-15 minutes.
In Season: Year-round.

Newport Scallops

by Laura & Chef Rob Biela

"I'll have a shot of Grandma..." is a common island refrain, with Grand Marnier, an orange rind liqueur, being Newport's toaster of choice. This scallop recipe is simple, healthy and delicious, using al-dente cauliflower to soak up the flavor rather than a starch.

The Catch

¾ pound 'dry' local Sea Scallops (approximately 1½ to 2 inches in diameter, ¾ inch thick)

The Groceries

1 Tablespoon canola oil
half a head of cauliflower
a shot of Grand Marnier
1 seedless orange or tangerine
1 heaping Tablespoon capers with 1 Tablespoon caper juice
a handful of flat parsley, chopped
1 Tablespoon cold butter

The How To

- PEEL the orange or tangerine into segments. If it doesn't happen neatly, that's no big deal. CUT the segments in half the short way. SET ASIDE with their juice.
- BREAK cauliflower into two inch wide florets, CHOPPING OFF any long stalks. RINSE and DON'T DRY, then PLACE in a microwave safe bowl, covered by an upside down microwave safe bowl. MICROWAVE on high for three minutes. LET SIT with bowl on top until needed.
- HEAT canola oil in skillet on high. (On gas stoves – non-stick skillets work as well as uncoated skillets. If using a non-stick skillet on an electric stove – you must get it radically hot and keep it so.)
- RINSE and DRY scallops with paper towel.
- When oil is hot enough for water to splatter, ADD scallops flat side down. COOK for 2½ minutes on medium high heat without disturbing them. Scallops will form a golden crust.
- FLIP scallops and COOK for two additional minutes on medium high without disturbing. There will be barely any oil left and that's fine. After two minutes, TEST one scallop by cutting it in half and confirming that the inside has very little translucency left. SET ASIDE scallops.
- DEGLAZE pan by adding a shot of Grand Marnier and scraping off anything stuck. Quickly REMOVE pan from heat and ADD scallops, capers with juice, orange pieces with juice, parsley and cauliflower. (SHAKE moisture off cauliflower before adding.)
- STIR IN cold butter and TOSS to distribute juices.
- SERVE immediately.

> **Fisherman's Tip:** If you are doubling this recipe, you might need to cook the scallops in batches. Don't crowd them.

Yield: Dinner for 2.
Kitchen Time: 15 minutes.
In Season: Year-round.

Red Curried Mussels

— Betty's way

Sometimes seafood lovers need a break from the 'regular' flavors of lemon, white wine and butter. This recipe uses three ingredients not found in every kitchen, (coconut milk, red curry paste, and fish sauce). But it's worth the supermarket scavenger hunt! It is so delicious, we've broken out straws to capture that last bit of broth!

The Catch
3-4 pounds mussels

The Groceries
2 Tablespoons canola oil
½ cup onion, diced
3-4 cloves of fresh garlic, minced
2 Tablespoons red curry paste
½ cup dry white wine
1 13-ounce can coconut milk
2 Tablespoons 'fish sauce'
2 Tablespoons brown sugar
2 Tablespoons fresh cilantro, minced
2 Tablespoons fresh basil leaves, thinly sliced
salt to taste

The Extras
crusty fresh bread

The How To

- CLEAN off mussels by adding 1 tablespoon of salt to a gallon of cold water. SOAK for about 30 minutes.
- SCRUB shells with a brush. REMOVE any beards present. (To debeard, pull at the seaweed/hair protruding from the shell until it releases. Do this right before cooking since the mussels will not live long after the de-bearding.)
- HEAT oil over medium heat in large pot.
- ADD onions and COOK until soft and semi-translucent, approximately 3-4 minutes.
- ADD garlic and COOK 1 minute.
- ADD curry paste and COOK 1 additional minute.
- ADD wine, coconut milk, 'fish sauce,' and brown sugar. SIMMER for approximately 5 minutes.
- ADD cleaned mussels, cilantro and basil. BRING to boil and STEAM covered 7 minutes.
- DISCARD any unopened mussels.
- SERVE mussels in bowls with plenty of broth and a loaf of crusty bread for soaking up broth. Straws optional...

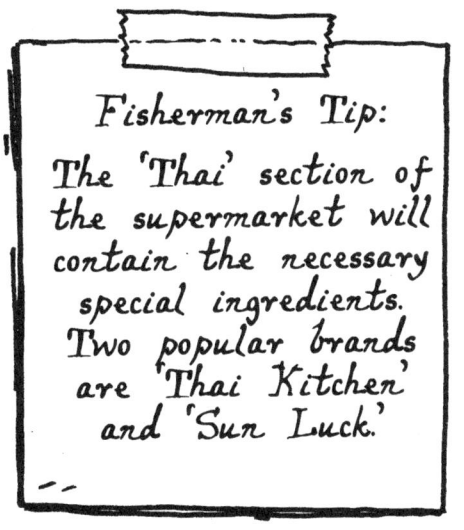

Fisherman's Tip: The 'Thai' section of the supermarket will contain the necessary special ingredients. Two popular brands are 'Thai Kitchen' and 'Sun Luck.'

Yield: Appetizer for 6. Dinner for 4.
Kitchen Time: Soak 30 minutes. Active 25 minutes.
In Season: Year-round.

Ricotta Stuffed Baby Squid

Squid is often stuffed with a breadcrumb mixture, but this Italian-inspired recipe uses the squid like noodles to hold rich ricotta cheese! Think, 'stuffed shells' but with squid's unique texture. This recipe is fun to do with kids, potentially messy, and satisfying. Make sure kids are in a good spot to watch as the squids 'inflate' in the sauté pan!

The Catch
1 pound cleaned squid tubes less than 5 inches long (Longer squid are too tough for this recipe.)

The Groceries
8 ounces ricotta cheese
1 egg
¼ cup grated parmesan cheese
4 leaves fresh basil, minced
½ teaspoon garlic powder
flour
¼ teaspoon black pepper
2 Tablespoons olive oil
2 cups marinara sauce

The Extras
1 pound linguine, if serving as meal
serrated steak knives

The Gear
toothpicks

The How To

- MIX ricotta, egg, parmesan and spices in medium size bowl.
- FILL a small ziplock bag with the mixture.
- SNIP a ¼ inch hole in a bottom corner of the bag.
- FIND a friend.
- STUFF the tubes half full: One person holds a tube's 'big end' open with two hands. The other person holds the stuffing bag and squeezes the stuffing into the tube gently. It helps to press the ziplock's hole right into the tube's opening. If you get carried away and fill them all the way they will explode...
- SEAL each tube roughly by threading a toothpick through the end.
- HEAT olive oil in sauté pan over medium.
- PREHEAT oven to 350°F.
- DUST each squid lightly with flour.
- SAUTÉ squids for about 1 minute per side until they 'puff up' into proud little balloons!
- PLACE squids in a 9 x 9 baking dish and cover with marinara.
- BAKE for 20 minutes at 350°F.
- SERVE with fresh bread, as an appetizer, or over linguine as an entrée. Serrated steak knives are helpful to slice through the squid without smushing out the stuffing. Watch out for toothpicks!

> ### Fisherman's Tip
>
> If you're cleaning the squid yourself, lay it flat, hold the end away from the head and press down with the back of the knife sort of the way you would 'curl' a Christmas ribbon. That should both squeeze the insides out and pull off the skin.

Yield: Appetizer for 4, or with pasta, a meal for 4.
Kitchen Time: Active 25 minutes. Bake 20 minutes.
In Season: Year-round.

Tequila Lime Grilled Calamari

Easy, elegant, unique. The smoky flavor of the barbeque with the delicate texture of calamari. The perfect 'side' to any barbeque.

The Catch

1 pound cleaned squid 'tubes' (Use the tentacles for something else as they tend to fall through the grill grate...)

The Groceries

1 lime, squeezed for juice
4 Tablespoons tequila
4 Tablespoons olive oil
4 cloves garlic, chopped
1 teaspoon oregano

The How To

- MIX lime juice, tequila, olive oil, chopped garlic and oregano in medium size container that has a cover and extra room. (Like a 5 cup Tupperware.)
- GET your kitchen scissors and your squid tubes.
- FIND the 'crease' running the length of each squid's tube. SNIP the tubes lengthwise along the crease to make flat sheets. CLEAN OFF anything that isn't white and smooth. IF any tubes are longer than 5 inches, CUT perpendicular to the crease to make them 2-3 inch segments.
- MIX squid and marinade well. COVER and REFRIDGERATE for 2+ hours, MIXING once or twice.
- HEAT grill to high and FIND tongs.
- SLAP each 'squid sheet' flat on the grill. GRILL for 2 minutes. They may 'curl up' into little rolls.
- FLIP with tongs and grill for 2 more minutes, encouraging them to curl up. (Cook longer if squids were longer than 5 inches, and therefore thicker.) If flesh isn't getting 'smoky' DRIP a little of the marinade on it to help the grill 'flame up.'
- SERVE immediately as an appetizer while they're still hot!

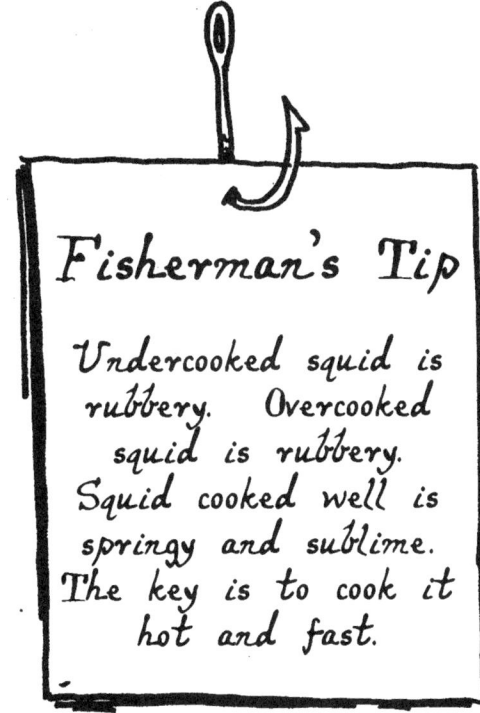

Fisherman's Tip

Undercooked squid is rubbery. Overcooked squid is rubbery. Squid cooked well is springy and sublime. The key is to cook it hot and fast.

Yield: Appetizer for 6.
Kitchen Time: Prep 10 minutes. Marinate 2 hours. Grill 4 minutes.
In Season: Year-round.

'Catch' from the Land...

The Local Catch

Aquidneck Island is generous with her fruits from the land, as well as the sea. A summer's stroll can yield a quart of sea-side blackberries while an October drive can result in a Jeep full of apples. Often the island creates these fruits on her own, without help or fertilizer -- it seems rude not to enjoy her gifts! In addition to wild offerings, there are island farms, farmers' markets and summer gardens to help you enjoy the fresh tastes of the land around you.

Local is fresh and fresh is best!

Farmers boil the water before they pick the corn for a reason – so that they can enjoy all that natural sugar before it turns to starch only minutes later. Soft 'farm strawberries' don't last long in the fridge, but their meat is a WOW. Sometimes the supermarket just can't measure up.

We've included a few dessert recipes that can be easily made with the local fruits of the land. If you don't have skills catching fish, maybe you should try berries. They don't swim very fast.

Bramble Cobbler 114
Rhubarb Crisp 116
Side-of-the-Road Apple Pie 118
Strawberry Shortcake 120
Very Blueberry Corn Muffins ...122

Bramble Cobbler

- adapted from a 'Gourmet Magazine' recipe for "Bill's Blueberry Cobbler," by Bill McDonald, Clinton, Minnesota, published in August 1998, and available on epicurious.com.

Huge blackberries or 'brambles' cover Aquidneck Island in late July. Abundant. Juicy. Delicious. Fat as grapes. This yummy 'cobbler' is so easy it's ridiculous.

The Catch
1 pint blackberries
　　aka 'brambles'

The Groceries
¾ stick butter (6 Tablespoons)

1 cup flour

2 teaspoons baking powder

½ teaspoon salt

½ teaspoon freshly grated nutmeg or cinnamon

1 cup sugar

⅔ cup milk

The Extras
vanilla ice cream

> *Fisherman's Tip:*
>
> *When harvesting island berries, wear gloves, pants and a long-sleeved shirt.*
>
> *They often grow near stinging nettles and poison ivy.*

The How To

- PREHEAT oven to 375°F.
- MELT butter in square baking dish (8-9 inch) in heating oven. REMOVE when melted.
- MIX dry ingredients in medium sized bowl.
- ADD milk and STIR with fork or whisk until just combined.
- POUR batter straight into the middle of the melted butter. Don't stir!
- DUMP berries straight into the middle of the batter. Don't stir! It should look like a pile of berries, sitting in a pile of batter, sitting in a pile of butter. (Yum!)
- BAKE for 40ish minutes until golden brown and the berries have exploded a little.
- SERVE straight up or with ice cream.

Yield: Dessert for 6.

Kitchen Time: Active 5 minutes. Bake 40 minutes.

Season: Late July - Early August.

Rhubarb Crisp

So many 'rhubarb' recipes get it wrong — hiding the zang of the rhubarb in a sea of mushy strawberries. So many 'crisp' recipes get it wrong with a soggy sweet topping that is anything but crispy. Never fear — Rhubarb Crisp is here, crunchily highlighting this local springtime treasure!

The Catch
6 cups fresh rhubarb, chopped (about 2 pounds)

The Groceries

For topping:

1 stick butter, melted

1 cup brown sugar, firmly packed

⅔ cup flour

1 cup oats (quick cooking or old fashioned...whatever)

⅔ cup chopped walnuts

1 teaspoon cinnamon

For filling:

2 Tablespoons flour

⅓ cup granulated sugar

1 teaspoon vanilla

The Extras
vanilla ice cream

The How To

- SET oven to 350°F.
- MELT a stick of butter in a mixing bowl.
- GREASE an 8-9 inch square baking pan and SPRINKLE a light layer of oats on the bottom. (This stops the filling from 'sticking' to the pan.)
- ADD brown sugar, flour, oats, nuts and cinnamon into butter bowl.
- MIX together until crumbly and try not to eat too much... SET ASIDE.

In a new bowl...

- MIX rhubarb, 2 tablespoons flour, $\frac{1}{3}$ cup sugar and vanilla together. DUMP into greased pan.
- COVER with oat mixture. PRESS down gently.
- BAKE at 350°F for 40-45 minutes. Rhubarb should be 'bubbly' and crisp should be deep golden brown.
- LET SIT for ten minutes to jell then SERVE UP with a spatula.
- TOP with vanilla ice cream!

Yield: Dessert for 8.

Kitchen Time: Active 10 minutes. Bake 45 minutes.

In Season: Late Spring.

Side-of-the-Road Apple Pie

Starting in late September, apples tumble to the side of the road all over the island. Mother Nature's bruised offerings might not always be perfectly pretty, but they make a pretty perfect pie! Brake for dessert!

The Catch

10-15 local apples
OR 6-8 store-sized apples
 (to make 4-5 cups of ¼ inch thick apple slices)

The Groceries

pie crust for 9 inch 2 crust pie
¾ cup sugar
2 Tablespoons flour
½ teaspoon cinnamon
dash nutmeg
5 pats of butter for top

The Extras

vanilla ice cream and/or cheddar cheese

The How To

- PEEL, CORE and SLICE apples (¼ inch thick) until you have 4-5 cups.
- COMBINE apples, sugar, flour and spices in a large bowl or pot with a lid and SHAKE SHAKE SHAKE!
- LINE 9 inch pie crust with bottom crust.
- DUMP seasoned apples into pie crust.
- ARRANGE 5 pats of butter on top of the apples in the configuration of a plus sign. This helps the top crust brown.
- SPREAD top crust over apples.
- ROLL the crusts' edges away from the center of the pie and PINCH together with your thumbs to seal.
- CUT generous steam slits in top for juices to bubble through.
- BAKE 50 minutes at 400 °F, or until juices bubble through the slits and the crust is golden brown. If crust edges brown too quickly, cover them with tinfoil to protect.
- LET STAND at least 10 minutes for juices to thicken. SERVE with ice cream, cheddar cheese or solo!
- THANK the 'Side-of-the-Road' store!

Fisherman's Tip

Put an old cookie sheet on the rack below your pie to catch messy drips.

Yield: Dessert for 8.

Kitchen Time: Active 30 minutes. Bake 50 minutes.

In Season: September-October.

Strawberry Shortcake

- adapted from the Bisquick website

Classic. Simple. What summer should taste like. Plenty of super juicy berries over a steaming hot buttery biscuit.

The Catch

2 pounds fresh picked strawberries

Fisherman's Tip

The 'green' cardboard container at a pick-your-own strawberry place holds about 1 pint of berries. To serve 6 people well, you really need two of those full containers.

The Groceries

½ cup sugar

2⅓ cups Bisquick

½ cup milk

3 Tablespoons sugar

3 Tablespoons butter melted

whipped cream OR vanilla ice cream

The How To

- REMOVE the leaves and SLICE the berries into a medium sized bowl. If they are local berries they won't have a white core. If they are supermarket berries they will; you can cut that out if you like as it doesn't have much taste.
- MIX in ½ cup sugar at least 30 minutes before you plan to eat (the longer the better!). LET SIT at room temperature and STIR every so often.

20 minutes before serving...

- HEAT oven to 425°F.
- MIX Bisquick, milk, 3 tablespoons sugar and melted butter in another medium bowl.
- FORM dough into 6 'patties' about 3 inches across. (If they're too wide, they're hard to split.) PLACE on ungreased cookie sheet.
- BAKE at 425°F for 10-12 minutes until tops are golden brown.
- SPLIT biscuits in half, COVER liberally with strawberries and juice.
- SERVE immediately with whipped cream or vanilla ice cream – or both!

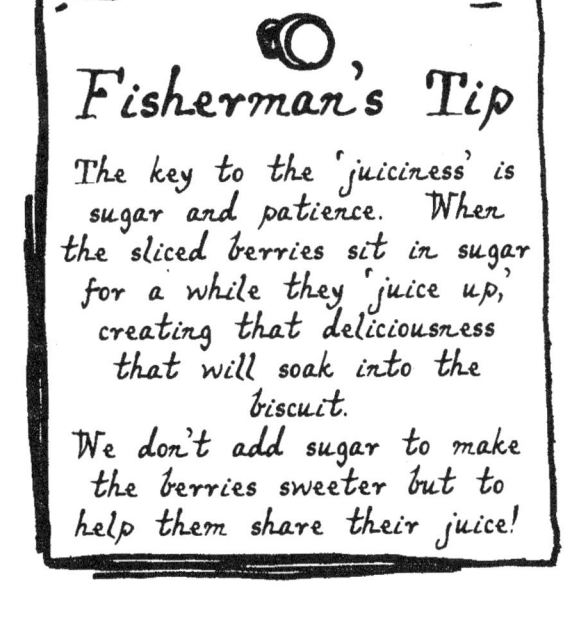

> **Fisherman's Tip**
>
> The key to the 'juiciness' is sugar and patience. When the sliced berries sit in sugar for a while they 'juice up,' creating that deliciousness that will soak into the biscuit.
> We don't add sugar to make the berries sweeter but to help them share their juice!

Yield: Dessert for 6.

Kitchen Time: Active 10 minutes. Wait 30 minutes. Bake 15 minutes.

In Season: Late June, early July.

Very Blueberry Corn Muffins

Blueberries are succulent, juicy and plentiful in summer at the island's farms...but sometimes blueberry muffins are dry and their berries sparse! Following the fisherman's style of more 'catch', less 'filler'...these muffins are what you always wanted a blueberry muffin to be.

The Catch
1 pint island blueberries, minus one big handful for a snack

The Groceries
1 package corn muffin mix (8½ ounces)
1 Tablespoon sugar
dash nutmeg
1 egg
⅓ cup milk
⅓ cup sour cream
2 packets raw sugar (or two Tablespoons regular)
cooking spray

The Gear
muffin tin for 8-9 muffins
paper muffin cups (these muffins are so juicy they have a hard time coming out of the pan!)

The How To

- HEAT the oven to 400°F.
- MIX muffin mix, sugar and nutmeg in a large bowl with a fork.
- STIR in egg, milk, sour cream and whole pint blueberries, minus handful for snacking.
- WAIT a couple minutes so it can do its thing.
- SPRAY muffin cups with cooking spray. One can't be too careful...
- STIR once and FILL muffin cups to top so they will crown. Try to get an even distribution of berries and batter...if one muffin ends up 'all berry' it will need to be eaten with a fork.
- SPRINKLE the raw sugar on top.
- BAKE at 400°F until golden brown and toothpick comes out free of dough. (About 20 minutes.)

Fisherman's Tip

Muffin papers are your friend.

Yield: 8-9 super-moist, berry-packed muffins!

Kitchen Time: Active 5 minutes. Bake 20 minutes.

In Season: 4th of July to Labor Day.

About the author...

Laura Blackwell lives, writes and harvests in Newport, RI. Her specialties are clams and berries, but she's been known to land a fish or two. One spring day she went searching for lobster on the State Pier and caught a handsome fisherman. They now cook their fresh catch together almost every night.
www.LauraBlackwell.com

About the illustrators...

Sean "Willis" Warren drew the page illustrations and back cover from his studio in world-famous Quincy, MA. He is a cartoonist by trade and, after this project, is committed to drawing only things which have eyes.

Mary Adiletta, the cover artist, gardens and digs clams in Westerly, Rhode Island. She swears by cutting clams with scissors.

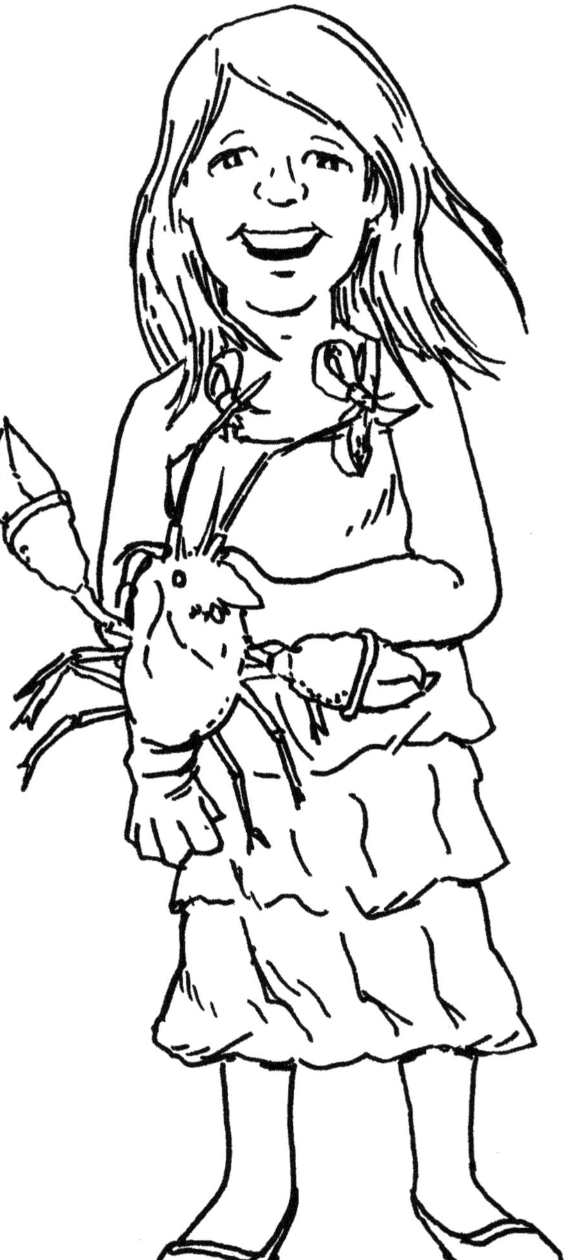

Thanks!

In no discernible order:

Gordon Tibbitts
Sean Warren
David Spencer
Denny Ingram
Russell Sylvestre
Eric Roggero
Mary & Mark Adiletta
Denise Oliveira
Bill Solitro
Robby Braman
Betty Blackwell
Mary Beth Blackwell
Bob Blackwell
Jenn Ferencko
Emily Coe
Deb Crowley
Peter Kosseff
Gail Ciampa

Linda & Brooks Thayer
Linnea Lundwall
Annie Sherman Luke
Dawn
Lawrence
Jack McCormack
Jeff & Sarah Harris
Amy & Jim Cordeiro
Trish Fisher
Ian Sylvestre
Ronnie & Jess McLeod
Christopher Francis Haas
Andrea Haas
Claire Ryan

AND
The Newport Lobster Shack
www.NewportLobsterShack.com

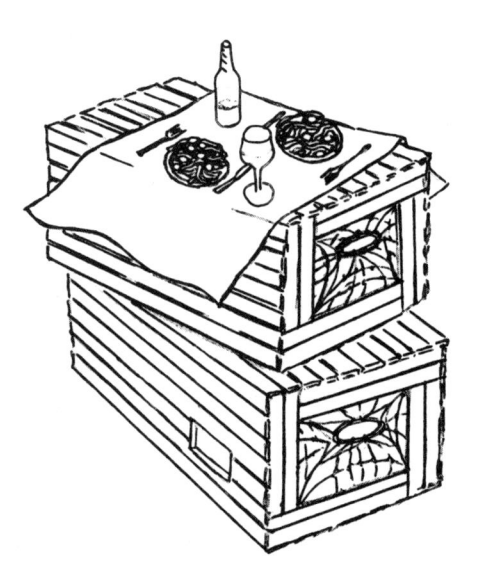

Visit
www.FishermansTable.com

for 'Video Recipes' like:

Lobster Ravioli in a Saffron Cream Sauce
and
Smoked Bluefish

as well as helpful "How To" videos like:

Scaling a fish
Cleaning a conch
and
Butterflying a lobster!

Enjoy the bounty of...

The Fisherman's Table!